# Aleister C

## A Modern Master

## by John Moore

## Placing the Beast in his Cultural Background

**Mandrake**

# Contents

# 0
# Introduction

If you are at all interested in modern occultism you will of course have come across Aleister Crowley, and what you have heard will not always have been good. 'Sinister' is one frequently applied epithet. Not that he himself would necessarily have minded that, after all he did cultivate a reputation as The Beast. Indisputably Crowley's life and work occupy a prominent, even if controversial, place within the occult tradition. Whether or not you approve of him, you only have to look at his books to appreciate the quality of his mind. His prose is at its best masterly. At the very least we can say, as Raoul Loveday said to Betty May in justification of his friendship, 'He is an extremely intelligent man'.[1]

Set beside other modern mystics and occultists like Gurdjieff, Ouspensky, Madame Blavatsky or Rudolf Steiner, Crowley acquits himself very well. In esoteric accomplishment he is what these were and much more. All of them aspired to an influence well beyond the byways of an occult subculture, and all succeeded to some degree. Nevertheless, while both Gurdjieff and Blavatsky in their own way achieved greatness and impacted on art and literature generally, it would not be appropriate to call them 'Modern Masters'. With Crowley it is, though his influence has been heavily downgraded or ignored, partly because the occult has such a lowly place in mainstream contemporary culture. Crowley is usually relegated to a tradition that is not to be taken seriously.

His life and teachings have been several times written. I have no wish to add to the number of such books. My aim is I believe original. I want to place him more squarely at the centre of things. Even, perhaps especially if you have little interest in the occult, Crowley deserves your attention. He applied his powerful intellect to engage with some of the most pressing issues of his own day, many of which remain as vital as ever. His Magick and his Thelema, outlandish as they might at first sound, are not just fringe ideas, they offer provocative answers and solutions to many of the urgent questions that still beset us. His message is meant for all, as he firmly states in the introduction to *Magick in Theory and Practice*. He challenged received opinion, which responded by cutting him out of serious history. Untangle his ideas from their bizarre sounding setting, and we can see how unjust was his exclusion. Most importantly, while received opinion has somewhat changed its character over the past sixty years, it is still powerfully subverted by the life and work of this badly underrated great man.

My object is to make Crowley intelligible in a mainstream context, to bring his creative achievement more into the light of sympathetic attention, make his ideas more accessible, and his religious outlook and experience available. This involves rewriting much recent intellectual history. The object is also to make excuses for him, defending what has been criticised as the more contemptible side of his character. While my main target audience is people who already know about Crowley and are intrigued enough to want to explore the context of his ideas, I am also writing for anyone interested in modern thought who is curious to discover if a case really can be made for his importance.

To describe his ideas as he explicitly set them out is definitely not the best path to understanding him. In the first place that would miss out the irony, the same quality he most prized in the writings of his previous incarnation.[2] If we ask the question what Crowley's ideas were, this is not easy to answer without creating misunderstanding. We might start to explain him by saying that he was a magus. You may ask why twenty-first century men and women should take any interest in this idea of a magus. As a magus, his idea is not so much the theoretical idea that 'one should be a magus', as the practical living this out. We can see his life's work as the culmination of a number of different traditions of continuing interest, such as Romanticism, Protestantism, philosophy and imperialism, which are of more than historical importance. Focus on these living traditions and Crowley's significance is clearly discernible.

Magick and mystery have not always been held in such low esteem. At various times in history magicians have been honoured and respected figures. We have only to think of the later Neo-Platonic movement, of Proclus, Iamblichus and their followers, and of the Platonism of the Italian Renaissance, Ficino, Pico and Bruno. Both of these eras preceded and followed what could be considered times of rationalism. In

Hindu society there was the period of the tantras. Nor even in much more recent times has the irrational been entirely expelled from the realm of respectable culture. In the nineteenth century there was Romantic decadence, and in the twentieth Surrealism. The poet Yeats, many of whose beliefs were every bit as bizarre as those professed by his one time associate, Crowley, is a much honoured figure. It can also be said, if we want to be strictly rational, that orthodox religious people let a good deal of irrationality into their view of the world.

The plan for this book was first conceived in 1984 as a contribution to the Fontana Modern Masters series. This was a series of paperbacks about the people who supposedly defined modernity, what is most creative and distinctive in the age in which we live. I felt strongly that Crowley deserved a place among these assorted gurus. It was annoying, reading much of what was taken so seriously and admired, that the writings of this unique genius should be so completely disregarded. Knowing the prejudice against him I didn't have any serious hope, but sent off a proposal all the same. I was told Crowley was not a suitable subject for inclusion. 'From a publishing point of view', I was told, he was 'simply too different from the other people we have included as subjects'. This was of course to be expected. Ezra Pound, high priest of modernism, had been adamant there should be no place for the Beast,[3] far preferring Crowley's nemesis, Mussolini.

I meant to show that Crowley is not so out of place in such company as is said. He was a significant presence in British culture between the wars, if not openly acknowledged. Most surveys of the twentieth century zeitgeist fail to include him. A creditable exception is Anthony Powell's great novel sequence *Dance to the Music of Time*, where a Crowley figure appears twice as a powerful dominating presence, early on as the cult leader Dr Trelawney and in the last book as his reincarnation, the charismatic young hippy Scorpio Murtlock.

## His Life

Aleister Crowley's life has been told many times, and fascinating as it is, there would be little point in repeating material that is easily available elsewhere. As an introductory framework I give this account, shorn of most of the amusing anecdotes that ornament his career. I would happily recommend any of the available biographies (except Colin Wilson's).[4]

On May 31st 1875 died Eliphas Levi, aka Alphonse Louis Constant, famous French magician, later averred to have been the previous incarnation of Edward Alexander Crowley, who was born on 12th October 1875 at Leamington Spa, Warwickshire, to Edward Crowley, a member of the Exclusive branch of the Plymouth Brethren, a fundamentalist Protestant sect, and his wife Emily Bertha, née Bishop.

After 1881 the family moved near Redhill in Surrey, where Aleister, as he was later to call himself, spent what he recalled as the happiest years of his childhood. In 1887 his father died and he moved with his mother to his uncle's house in Drayton Gardens, South Kensington. His uncle, though not a Plymouth

Brother, was nevertheless a narrow-minded religious prig who was to fuel Aleister's loathing of Christianity.

He was sent to school at Malvern and Tonbridge. In 1895 he went up to Trinity in Cambridge, the college which was once able to boast that it had won more Nobel prizes than France. His student days were spent at the height of the decadent era. His best friend at Cambridge was an amateur female impersonator, Jerome Pollitt, with whom he had an apparently homoerotic relationship and was to break on account of Pollitt's pessimistic philosophy of life. Through Pollitt he met Aubrey Beardsley.

At Cambridge he published the first of his many volumes of poetry and began his long career of adventurous travel.

Leaving Cambridge, he became an accomplished mountaineer with his friend Oscar Eckenstein. Following their failed attempt on K2, the second highest mountain in the world, for a number of years he held a number of world records, including that for the longest time spent at such a high altitude. This consideration might arguably make us more receptive to his claims to other sorts of record, such as those relating to spiritual attainment.

He was introduced to the Golden Dawn, an influential occult order which attracted a number of prominent people. If we think of its rituals as an advanced form of Freemasonry that should make them seem less bizarre than they otherwise do to modern minds unfamiliar with such practices. The subculture of the occult offered a vehicle for all sorts of excluded ideas.

For a while he was closely associated with S L (Macgregor) Mathers, disputed head of the order, whose flamboyant occultist persona Crowley is said (as by Symonds) to have imitated in several respects.

In the Golden Dawn also he met Allan Bennett, who taught him magic, and who by Crowley's financial assistance was enabled to become a Buddhist monk in Ceylon and Burma, later returning to become a proselytiser for Buddhism in the West. Together with Bennett, Crowley experimented widely with psychotropic drugs, a practice which he was to continue throughout his life, perfectly legally for the first part of it. With Bennett's aid he also pursued a serious study of Yoga and Buddhism, which he was to extend into other oriental spiritual traditions.

His poetry won the admiration of the young Captain (later General) J F C Fuller who proclaimed the new religion of Crowleyanity. Crowley's poetry was his first bid for fame and success, and on balance that can be judged a failure. Fuller notwithstanding, his critical acclaim was limited. He had a lot of compelling ideas and opinions he was very concerned to communicate, but he had not yet found the right medium for doing this.

The medium he did settle upon he was to call Magick (sic). In Boleskine, a house he bought on the shores of Loch Ness, he began the magickal operation for the attainment of the knowledge and conversation of the Holy Guardian Angel, following the instructions given in *The Book of Sacred Magic of Abra Melin the Mage.*

In 1903 he married Rose, sister of his friend Gerald Kelly. She was the first of the many 'scarlet women' who filled his life. For some people his sexual success is the main measure of his greatness. He had a vast number of sexual partners, including men and prostitutes. He claimed it was the androgyny in his make up that enabled him to understand women and 'emerge from the battle of sex unscathed'. Unfortunately Rose came to a bad end, like many of those who were close to him.[5]

In 1904, while travelling with Rose there took place what Crowley considered the central event of his career, the Great Revelation in Cairo, where he received the sacred scripture *The Book of the Law.* The fundamental message of this document was Thelemism, summed up in the adage *"Do What Thou Wilt shall be the whole of the law."*

*The Book of the Law* is in three parts. It reads like possession, via a messenger, Aiwass, by the personalities of three primordial Egyptian deities in turn, Nuit, Hadit and his son Ra Hoor Khuit. Together with Ra Hoor Khuit there is Hoor par Kraat, Harpocrates, who of necessity remains silent. He is the brother of Ra Hoor Khuit.

So far we have five beings. Then there is the Beast, not necessarily identified with Crowley himself, and his Scarlet Woman. The Beast is the prophet, and the Scarlet Woman presumably his shakti, his yum. Thus there are seven beings. With the scribe this makes eight.

Aiwass is said to be the cosmic intelligence that receives this system. He is the focal point giving unity to the whole conception. The message is not quite the same in each part. There are three distinct personalities, though father and son can be difficult to distinguish.

Much of the circumstances surrounding its reception parallel mental illness. There are the miraculous coincidences, the proofs and confirmations that are not really evident to an outside observer. Yet Crowley was far from mad.

In the following year he led an expedition to ascend Kanchenjunga, which ended in disaster. This brought him a degree of obloquy in mountaineering circles.

He spent the First World War in America where he wrote propaganda for Germany in periodicals called *The International* and *The Fatherland*. There has been some controversy over whether he really was the traitor he appeared to be, or was working undercover for the British secret services.

After his return, he met Victor Neuberg, a young Jewish poet with whom he conducted some very intense sexual Magick, particularly an operation in the Algerian desert, based on the system of Enochian Calls developed by the Elizabethans John Dee and Edward Kelly.

In 1920 he founded a magickal community in the Sicilian village of Cefalu, called the Abbey of Thelema. His Scarlet Woman at this time was Leah Hirsig, known as Alostrael. Leah who died in obscurity and apparent failure,[6] deserves to be honoured as one of the most remarkable women of the twentieth century. If Crowley was great she shared in his greatness, because she understood him and threw herself wholeheartedly into her role. She became the best of all the Scarlet Women, attaining for the Thelemite the glory of an incarnate goddess.

He brought to the Abbey the man he considered his best ever student, the brilliant young Raoul Loveday, his appointed heir or Magickal son. When they met in London, Raoul was involved with a young woman with a colourful past, Betty May, who was not happy with the association with Crowley. She wrote about her experiences in an autobiography, *Tiger Woman*. Raoul tragically died at the Abbey from drinking infected water, against Crowley's explicit warning.

The Abbey made some demands on its members. The drugs were meant to be taken in a self-disciplined way for spiritual development. Crowley was conducting his life in the way he wanted, living out some of his ideas. The rules were not particularly oppressive, nor was there brainwashing. Thelemism should not be seen as a cult. The Abbey was a place for intelligent conversation and refined enjoyment. Betty emphasises Crowley's taste for fine wine. From Crowley's point of view, a lot of people were interested in him and this living together in a community enabled such an interest to develop itself. Modern society still objects to such experiments in living. Intolerance remains. Anyone who tried to live like that now would still be persecuted.

High minded as it may have been, the Abbey experiment has to be judged a failure, partly because of the death, but also the addictions and other psychological casualties that ensued.

Following a sustained and venomous campaign against him in the British popular press, Mussolini finally expelled Crowley and his followers from Italy in 1923.[7] To his later regret Crowley did not attempt to sue Lord Beaverbrook, owner of the *Sunday Express,* as he had been advised to do.

In 1934 he brought the unsuccessful libel action which was his downfall and brought about his bankruptcy. When he sued Nina Hammett for a fairly innocuous remark in her autobiography *Laughing Torso,* he was arguably suffering from that distortion of judgement that is an effect of prolonged cocaine use.

Fuller was not the only one to have seen a parallel between Crowley and Christ. Immediately after his defeat a nineteen year old girl came up to him, told him the verdict was the wickedest thing since the crucifixion and offered to become the mother of his child, which she did.

On 1st December 1947 he died, so having managed to exceed his three score years and ten. Symonds lived much longer, but three other of his biographers had untimely deaths, Francis X. King (1939–1994) Martin Booth (September 7, 1944 - February 12, 2004) and Gerald Suster (1951-2001).

Crowley's most lasting achievement is the body of literature he has left behind him in which he expresses the most fascinating and diverse ideas. His writing is uneven however - his poetry as well as his prose.

Here is some of the best of Crowley. This is far from a complete bibliography. In trying to select the masterpieces it is hard to pare it down:-

*Magick in Theory and Practice* - One of the great books of the twentieth century, a textbook of Magick addressed to all. *The Book of Lies* - Recognised by himself and others as a masterpiece, best described as poems, prose and verse in which he manages to achieve a concision absent from much of his Browningesque longer verse. *Liber Aleph, or the book of Wisdom or Folly* - Short essays of practical advice addressed to his magickal son. *The Confessions-* his autobiography. *Liber Legis with commentaries* aka - *The Book of the Law*. *The New Comment* is interesting but not necessarily reliable. *The Gospel according to George Bernard Shaw-* His very interesting understanding of the origins of Christianity. *The Holy Books* - These are among the very best things he wrote, like *Liber Legis* in some ways, but without the proclamation of a law. To some they are the perfection of mystical experience expressing the associated difficulties and dangers in a modern form, better than anything from orthodox religion. *Magick without Tears* - A very late work, with more of his very profound and interesting thoughts and observations.

For nearly twenty years after his death Crowley was generally disdained or reviled. Nevertheless he was steadily acquiring a widening circle of admirers, and at the end of the 1960s he was acclaimed as one of the heroes of the new counterculture.[8] For a while his greatness was taken almost at his own estimation.

By the beginning of the new millennium, after pop and postmodernism, Crowley's place in the history of culture ought to be secure. Things are not as bad as they were a couple of decades ago, and he has at last found his rightful place in the National Portrait Gallery. He is fully qualified to take his place as a Modern Master in the very diverse company of Camus, Mcluhan, Jung, Artaud,[9] Lenin, Chomsky, Gandhi, Yeats, Wittgenstein, Eliot and the rest, but the case still needs to be made. It is now sixty years after his death, and my book is completed, with the same chapter headings as originally conceived. For his full appreciation a lot of background was needed. I hope I have succeeded in supplying that.

The depth and variety of ideas discussed, and the original perspectives, make Crowleyana the sort of literature that people will want to return to again and again, to dip into and reread.

That has been my own experience with Crowley, both his own writings and books about him. To any particular person at any particular time some passages will be more interesting than others. Other people, as well perhaps as the same person earlier or later, will have a different focus.

# Notes

1   May, Betty, *Tiger Woman* p. 139
2   See his translation of Levi's *Key of the Mysteries* p. 22 where he praises his 'sublime irony'.
3   He reprimanded Mencken, the great American critic, for showing an interest in Crowley. (Sutin 2002 p. 243)
4   This is not to say that Wilson has not written several other books of value and interest
5   She died of alcoholism in 1932.
6   In *The King of the Shadow Realm*, (p. 405) Symonds says she died in 1951. Other authorities put her death as 1975 in Switzerland.
7   Crowley attacks Mussolini in *Songs for Italy* straightforwardly as a tyrant, on the basis of traditional ideas of liberty.
8   "Behold the great Crowley and tremble!", proclaimed the underground magazine *International Times* (October 5th - 20th 1967).
9   Artaud, significantly, wrote prophecies much in the style of Crowley.

# 1
# Crowleyan Romanticism

His biographers and expositors have taken various different approaches to Crowley's teachings. There is Symonds who curiously denies all value to them, Cammell who praises him as a poet but abhors the law of Thelema, Fuller who hails him as the new Christ, Regardie who treats his teachings as psychology, Francis King who explains his message in terms of sex magick and the religion of Thelema. None of these approaches quite manage to articulate the real nature of his appeal.

One accessible route to a sympathetic understanding of Crowley is the tradition of Romanticism, which is familiar enough. In expressing the unappeasable urge for the apparently unattainable, the romantic movement is the modern western equivalent of the magic and mysticism of the civilisations of the past. Romanticism is one of the great movements of the western mind. Its origin is generally placed around the middle of the eighteenth century. Arguably it still dominates today, attempts to move beyond it most often springing from Romantic motives themselves. It should be thought of as a form of consciousness or sensibility rather than a philosophy, though there are what can be called Romantic philosophies. It was originally a reaction against eighteenth century Rationalism. Against the cold constraints of Rationalism Romantics prize the joy of yielding to the fascination of innumerable different ideas while remaining inwardly free.

Aleister Crowley is the consummation of a certain phase of Romanticism. His apparent absurdity is like that of the physical element in Christianity, or of the psychedelic hallucination. The triumph over the transcendent is the supreme exemplification of the law of Thelema. It is the proclamation of the impossible, the miraculous. In *Magick without Tears* Crowley grudgingly commends Cardinal Newman for writing how as a child he used to wish the *Arabian Nights* were true,[1] and himself asserts in one of his most serious statements, that this wish is fully attainable.

From this viewpoint, Crowley's masterpiece is his *Magick in Theory and Practice*. As he writes in the introduction, this book is 'for all',[2] that is to say it is not directed at any specialised public. This sober description of how to fulfil the wildest, most extravagant ambitions is one of the great books of the twentieth century, a Romantic masterpiece superseding Eliphas Levi's nineteenth century equally romantic popularisation of the magical tradition. Popularisation bestows an entirely new dimension on the subject. Magic as an esoteric pursuit on the farthermost fringes of the public creed, is a very different matter from the same thing publicly proclaimed as a contribution to the mainstream higher culture of the day.

The Platonism of the Renaissance, which inspired much of the greatest art and literature of the sixteenth and early seventeenth centuries, was succeeded by a form of Rationalism known as the Enlightenment, or the 'Age of Reason'. Philosophies prevailed which judged the objectives and purposes of human life according to a predetermined standard of rationality. Romanticism may be interpreted as a revolt against this. It conjures up a great fund of emotion.

Romantic art and literature expressed all kinds of apparently irrational forces and anarchic instincts, which the Enlightenment had preferred to ignore, and in so doing implied the inadequacy of the Rationalistic schemes as a whole account of human nature. As a revolt against Rationalism, Romanticism in a sense presupposes it by reasserting the material left over by that system. Romanticism contrasts with Rationalism, it rebels against the limitations on experience imposed by a supposedly rational plan of existence. Rationalism can take many forms. Each claims a certain inevitability and authority. Different forms of Romanticism arise, in reaction to different forms of Rationalism. It is not an attack on reason itself. Crowley's Romanticism did not exclude his Rationalism.

To call something Romanticism can sometimes be to belittle it. Romanticism is old hat, everyone wants to be something more original. And I would not want to imply that Crowley was a *mere* Romantic. Crowley's mysticism is not reaction, not pose or style. It looks forward to a completely new form of Rationalism, taking place in the context of a wide range of emotional experience, Romantic, post-Romantic, pre-Romantic, un-Romantic, etc.

One aspect of the Romantic movement was pagan revival. The Age of Reason was only weakly pagan, as we can see from a poem like Gray's *Hymn to Adversity*. Though inspired by Aeschylus' observation that *"A man must suffer to be wise"*, the poem lacks all tragic sense. It is complacent because it takes too much for granted, it presupposes the protection of refined civilisation, it confronts neither fear nor real suffering. Nothing is taken seriously anymore, fundamental problems have ceased to exist, a polite culture has so to speak 'solved' them. This is the world of Ovid and Lord Chesterfield. This kind of culture flourishes best under a despotism, as Augustan Rome or Bourbon France. Freedom brings challenges and an art to tackle them, as Milton had attempted. The Satan of *Paradise Lost* was a hero for the Romantics, bringing a diabolic strain into the movement.

In the *Confessions* Crowley said he had never read Boswell[3] and he showed little interest in Dr Johnson. Johnson is sometimes cited as an example of the pre-Romantic, or Rationalist attitude. It is intimated that he was, perhaps, like the pagans before Christianity, missing something of vital importance, that his preference for the city and dislike of mountains indicates a constriction of taste, almost as if the Romantics were to bring psychic health into the world. Actually he was quite aware of the possibility of proto-Romantic attitudes, and he applied reason fair-mindedly to discuss the merits of different ways of looking at things. Dr Johnson's opinions were controversial and individual, anything that made such an outlook impossible would be a retrograde step.

The proto-Romantic mid eighteenth century was a era of exceptionally high energy. It should not be thought that esoteric traditions could not flourish at such a time. Sir Francis Dashwood of Hell Fire fame foreshadowed much in Crowley from a pre-Romantic era, the pleasure loving mid-eighteenth century. From the same period came R Payne Knight's alternative conception of the perennial philosophy in his *Essay on the Worship of Priapus*[4] which is very attractive. It was arguably the Romantics who really lost for us the ancient esoteric, Neo-Platonic tradition. In presupposing Enlightenment even while reacting against it, they lost immediate access to a lot of past thought forms.

It was not so much the Enlightenment that killed the esoteric tradition as Romanticism itself. The culture of the Enlightenment was aware of such ideals, much as it might have opposed them; the Romantics turned to them second-hand, as to something opposed to rationalism, and changed their meaning. Romanticism was the victory of Enlightenment culture, the first movement to presuppose it. Everything outside it was treated as bizarre and exotic, but the reasons for desiring the bizarre and exotic were rational and intelligible.

Much Romanticism had a suicidal aspect, well symbolised by Napoleon's attack on Russia. Romanticism may expend itself and forget the conditions of its own achievement. It contains the seeds of its own destruction, an impulse to overcome itself and turn into something else.

Crowley's Romanticism extended to a strong admiration for Shelley, which brought him into sympathy with the poet's revolutionary enthusiasm. Paradoxically this highly Romantic poetry was attached to a supposedly Rationalist system, that of William Godwin.

Here is one critic writing in 1913:-

> "The supremacy of an intellectual vision is not a common characteristic among poets, but it raises Milton and Shelley to the choir in which Dante and Goethe are leaders. ... to Shelley Political Justice was the veritable 'milk of Paradise'. We must drink of it ourselves if we would share his banquet. Godwin in short explains Shelley, and it is equally true that Shelley is the indispensable commentary to Godwin. For all that was living and human in the philosopher he finds imaginative expression."[5]

The altruistic and egalitarian impulse of Shelleyan idealism may seem quite different from the Byronic spirit which was selfish and aristocratic. The Byronic was another face of the movement. On such a ground Bertrand Russell (in *History of Western Philosophy*) was hostile to romanticism, seeing it as egoistic, anarchistic, sadistic, intrinsically amoral.[6] Romanticism as Russell saw it is something having very broad implications. We might see it sympathetically as something of religious significance, the European response to the death of religion, a way of making life exciting as it was for the earliest men on the plains of Africa. Existentialism, with its concepts of authentic and inauthentic existence is merely one of the most modern of Romantic positions.

Popular Romanticism obviously and naturally would not long sustain a note of aristocratic egoism. Romanticism had in it a strain of self-indulgence which easily led to sentimentality, originally egoistic, but ending up as a straightforward coarsening of ordinary morality. If we never read the bad literature of the past in addition to the good, we can hardly compare other eras with our own. And when we do compare we wonder what we have now in place of Romanticism. Life has become fragmented, our popular literature appeals to particular lusts.

Those attracted to the more Byronic and Nietzschean side of Crowley may find it hard to sympathise with his Shelleyan idealism. With the latter goes free love, equality, communism even, the perennial dreams of millenarian fantasy. Sometimes the element of sentimentality in Romanticism led it away from individualism into the realm of black and white fables, and on to the moral oversimplifications that comprise modern socialism.

Shelleyan idealism was one possible idea. It certainly did not hold Crowley captive. As he writes in *The Book of Lies*, "I am not an anarchist in your sense of the word."[7]

He explores some forms of experience which involve the complete antithesis of freedom. Every value, every idea, can be negated. This does not contradict Thelema, it is a consequence of it. People like Nietzsche and Crowley constantly change their minds but we can read their different statements together and find wisdom in the combination. This is to go deep into esoteric reading. Saying something which contradicts and therefore disturbs is giving a contrary point of view which needs to be considered. Changes of mind are read and perhaps should be read as if they are consistent. The magical balancing of ideas helps to explain the interest of the Shelleyan side. In the opposite is the disturbing, it keeps us in mind of our limited understanding like the admonitions of the Sufi master. Magical balance taken on its own may seem to lead to complete confusion. Have we moved beyond it?

The original Romantic reaction was repeated several times over in the course of the next century in response to successive stages of popularisation and vulgarisation. Thus came Symbolism, Decadence and Modernism. A reaction in itself only provides a convention, a form within which individual inspiration can operate. The Rationalism against which Romanticism reacts involves the claim that certain particular patterns of feeling and behaviour are given by reason, and therefore possess authority over us. The restrictiveness of this viewpoint is rejected by the Romantic with the force of revelation.

As Romanticism evolved, it developed into the so called decadent movement of the later nineteenth century. Late Romantics like Baudelaire, Mallarmé, Flaubert, Lautréamont, Swinburne, we may even include Dostoyevsky, took the interest in the perverse to extreme, sometimes dangerous, limits. The fatal man (Byron) was succeeded by the fatal woman. Crowley makes an appearance in Mario Praz's *Romantic Agony* (1930) as an extreme example of a decadent poet who '*later devoted himself to the practice of black magic*'.[8] Praz quotes some lines from *Jezabel* by way of illustration, which conclude:-

". . . Now let me die to mate in hell
With thee O harlot Jezabel."

The history of Romanticism was a clamour for escape as well as a demand for happiness. There is a greater sense of life that it succeeds in transmitting for a while particularly through the vehicle of hero worship. Yet what it produces is not permanent. Little remains, we stay frustrated. It is not altogether the message that is liberating.

One expresses discontent with the prevailing culture when forced to confront its oppressive limitations. The Romantics objected to the constraints of Rationalism, the Decadents objected to popular culture, and the twentieth century avant garde objected to the consumerisation of everything. Both the avant garde and the Decadents were hostile to a pseudo rationalism associated with political and economic forces. The old Rationalism of the Enlightenment suffered numerous vulgarisations and transmutations with the democratisation of society. Also with rationalisation Romanticism itself lost its fire and became reasonable.

The Symbolist movement of the later nineteenth century can be seen as a rationalisation of the escapist element in Romanticism. According to the Symbolists there exists another world, another plane of consciousness, more satisfying and pleasurable than mundane reality. Crowley is situated in both traditions. He identified fully with the rebellious impulses of Shelley and Blake as well as being fully immersed in the tradition of late nineteenth century Decadence.

He included Richard Wagner as one of his Gnostic saints.[9] Wagner's music represents a consummation of nineteenth century Romanticism, the coming together of all sorts of themes, from fascinating Decadence and degeneration to the philosophy of Schopenhauer. Crowley's own *Tannhauser*, with its Wagnerian theme, he regarded as one of the most important of his poems and put on his reading list. He called it his own *Pilgrim's Progress*.[10]

Charles Baudelaire, poet of Satanism and the perverse, it is said, did not really know much of Wagner, but according to Nietzsche, who knew a great deal, he was his first intelligent critic. Crowley's Great Whores owe as much to him as to the *Book of Revelation*. Crowley was a Decadent, like the Symbolists who followed Baudelaire. He was concerned to explore the fascination of the most supposedly decadent and degenerate ideas and to yield to them in luxurious experiment. Wagner's corrupt civilisation is something to be enjoyed, just like the decadence denounced in the Bible.

What first appeals to many about Crowley is his extreme romantic absurdity. Magic strikes us as self gratifying nonsense. Orthodox critics may deride, as Praz wrote of 'Sar' Peladan, "*However fantastic and absurd it may sound, Peladan devoted himself very seriously to the practice of Magic.*"[11] Modern magick was a delightful triumph of the surreal and the absurd. This is especially clear if we take seriously a simpler book than *Magick,* such as *Book 4,* which presents a magickal system in a classic form. There is a naïve purity in this primer, though Crowley's strange mind still comes strongly through. Some of what he says is on the face of it hardly acceptable and seems to contradict what we have taken to be his central message. Sometimes, for example, he seems to advocate the most absolute servitude to the arbitrary superstition. He uses his dogmatic authority to play jokes on his followers. But where do the jokes end? Sometimes he seems to abuse his authority. As in his expressed admiration for the Jesuits, there seems to be a spiritual sadism, a perverse delight in the most constricted.

He used to speak of "*the vision of the demon Crowley.*" It is not difficult to grasp what he meant by that. In a note in *Tannhauser* he writes "*It is a tradition of magic that all words have a double effect; an upright and an averse.*" If he abuses his position, issuing his thought experiments as ripened fruits of wisdom, is it because he knows that it would ultimately do no harm to follow even the most absurd and negative injunctions, on the principle of the union of opposites? But all this can be very confusing.

There is much beauty to be found in the system of ceremonial magic and its symbolism, even a religion of aesthetic sublimity. Nevertheless Crowley sets up immense barriers to his understanding. He befogs and bemuses. His speculations are fascinating, even when it is hard to see how they fit together. Sometimes they are traps for those who yearn to submit themselves to despotic authority. He may not appear to have achieved a grand coordinated system. Much of what he did is marred by faults of style.

A system of Magick can be taken as a way of training the will to equip it for any kind of experience, expressed in whatever language. Magick holds out the hope for the realisation of all Romantic hopes and ambitions, while keeping hold of the world of common sense. Yet it is guarded with supernatural terrors. There are what look like insuperable difficulties and much seeming unpleasantness to protect against misunderstanding and vulgarisation. The law of Thelema is for the few and secret.

The limitations of a non-Romantic, effectively Rationalistic interpretation of Crowley's achievement is apparent in the work of Israel Regardie, his one time secretary. As well as a Thelemite, Regardie was a devoted follower of the wayward psychoanalyst Wilhelm Reich. His book on Crowley, *The Eye in the Triangle* is in its own way most impressive. He emphasizes the importance of the Golden Dawn. However his whole notion of mystical progress is highly questionable. Crowley's crossing of the Abyss was indeed a personal psychological development, but it is stretching the point to imply this makes him the Superhero or vastly superior being that is suggested. If you move in the right circles, it is not unusual to meet people who have crossed the Abyss, hardened drug fiends who claim to have destroyed the personality. The whole Golden Dawn system is a poetic fiction, a framework within which you may have experience. There is no goal, it is a lot of playacting at times no doubt, and good pagan stuff to be sure, but the theory of initiations, the discovery of ever more profound trances, cannot be the significance of Crowley's life's work. Regardie treats the mysticism psychologically as if Crowley were in reality a discoverer of important psychological truths, a kind of Freud or Jung, if perhaps a bit more of an all rounder, one justified by truth.

Taking the thread of the Golden Dawn initiations he discovers the key to a Jungian-Reichian doctrine of psychic development and integration. Both Reich and Jung were psychological elitists. For both of them integration is known to only the rarest of the rare. Rarer still is that stray genius who knows how to communicate such integration, who has a way of teaching it. But if we are talking poetic fiction, it is arguable that all Crowley teaches is a fantasy of integration. If that is so, it may still have great value, but it could hardly be his real message. You are free to take him as an example to illustrate your ideas if you see fit to do so, but those ideas will not be what he was really trying to say.

If we accept that Crowley's real message was the *Book of the Law* that changes everything. Before that he was primarily a poet. We might also see him as a mystic. There are different kinds of mystics. Mystics old style were concerned with the discovery of an ultimate truth. Regardie writes that *"That Crowley was illuminated there can be no doubt whatsoever."*[12] How could we understand this? There is a natural tendency to treat as realities our own projected emotions. What is an illuminated person? We can make an analogy with the word 'beloved'. Imagine someone speaking of 'the beloved' as if a right understanding of the object of his love would arouse the same emotion in everyone. To say Crowley was illuminated is to say that he was capable of inspiring a certain emotional response in people, or that he does so in you. It is not to say that he had certain experiences.

Think of the various forms that the quest for illumination might take. Suppose it is conceived as a definite quality that is embodied in some particular (charismatic) person, like Hitler, Jesus, Buddha, Bhagwan, Crowley. What are you after if you seek illumination? To acquire that quality for yourself? To undergo certain experiences? To impress others? To gain an imperturbable wisdom? To undergo an experience which will automatically bestow all these things? It is possible that your progress might be hampered by a confusion between quite separate things. The object itself does not necessarily carry the emotional charge that you have given it. The charge and the object are separable. Loss of ego, crossing the Abyss, reduced to psychology is a technique, nothing momentous, certainly not of philosophical importance.

Like Salvador Dali, Crowley felt the necessity of outrageousness, to flout conventional morality. One could defend him, as against Regardie (who criticises him more than I think he feels inclined) on sufistic lines.[13] The Sufi master tries to shock people out of their conventional ways. Crowley had wealth and connections and consequently was able to exercise a lot of power. This included the power so visibly to flout taboos. Regardie does not always appear to appreciate the springs of this need to outrage. Should we say it is part of a mystical vision? But what is mysticism? Does every mystic have to have regular visions?

Crowley refined on occult concepts found in Blavatsky and elsewhere. His disappearing adepts are a most attractive and even useful conception. Esoteric doctrines come in many forms, some highly romantic. So often what truth there is comes with a vast superstructure of what seems irrelevant nonsense. One might feel this about Gurdjieff and Ouspensky. Crowley is different, he expands our awareness into all philosophy, all religious conceptions. Moreover he does not always mean what he says.

We can treat Crowley's concepts as works of art. The beauties are not perceptible to everyone. Perhaps it requires early exposure to see them and form the taste. His are unofficial ideas such as are not studied in universities. In a passage in the *Confessions* he describes how disgustingly tame he found the cultural atmosphere of his own time.

> "In reading Mr. Lytton Strachey's Eminent Victorians, and still more his Queen Victoria, as also in discussing periods with the younger generation, I find total failure to appreciate the attitude of artists and advanced thinkers who remember her jubilee. They cannot realize that to us Victoria was sheer suffocation ... And yet, somehow or other, the spirit of her age had killed everything we cared for. Smug, sleek, superficial, servile, snobbish, sentimental shopkeeping had spread everywhere ... It was impossible to dynamite the morass of mediocrity. Progress was impossible. The most revolutionary proposals, the most blasphemous theories, lost their sting. ..England had become a hausfrau's idea of heaven, and the empire an eternal Earl's Court exhibition . . . "[14]

Such feeling drove his creative efforts together with those of the other artists and advanced thinkers with whom he identified at this period. Looking back on that era we may remember their achievements more than the evil they were designed to overcome. One who feels mutatis mutandis an equivalent loathing for Blairite Britain (I write in 2007) may look for comparable remedies. Despite what its journalists would like us to think, the quality of an era is not all captured in newspapers. Looking in retrospect, the 1890s may seem to offer a certain imaginative satisfaction. Inspired by this one might imagine a new society which provided a comparable solace. In contemplation we see some of the fruits of the era. Insofar as our culture has abandoned Romanticism it does not seem to have embraced anything better. Oppressive so called rationality and coercive moral despotism, mutadis mutandis, remain in place. The price of worldly success is still compromise. If Romantic images can no longer be generated that may be because people are expected to be satisfied with far less. There is not the drive, the discontent, to create a depth culture, only a surface one.

Whatever we think of their philosophic base, Romanticism and Decadence at least stood for an attitude to life. After the First World War there was from this point of view a clear regression, even if certain excesses needed to be counteracted and satirised. The focus moved right away from the fulfilment of the exceptional individual. There was a reaction against the entire Romantic movement, yet not back into pre-Romantic Enlightenment synthesis, certainly not to the proto-Romantic or the Renaissance ideal, rather to something earlier and less sympathetic, something of the atmosphere of the mediaeval cloister. One of the motives was a desire to preserve the sense of being a cultural elite. Crowley's own sensibility became sidelined. His footnote to his remarks on Victorian England suggested that things later got even worse. "And in 1929 I find myself rather regretting those 'spacious days!' ' "[15]

For Crowley to have changed the world, or at least England, there were some missed opportunities. Beatrice Hastings, the South African adventuress, later to become Modigliani's mistress and model, sabotaged one chance. *The New Age* edited by Alfred Orage was the most influential literary periodical of its time, and even had a significant influence on the early days of the Labour Party. This is from *Alfred Orage and the Leeds Arts Club*, 1893-1923 by Tom Steele:-

> "Orage was later taken up with Aleister Crowley, the beast himself, who was briefly leader of the order [Golden Dawn] and according to Beatrice Hastings would have filled *The New Age* pages with his turgid outpourings had she not prevented him. Ms Hastings, a brilliant though erratic talent, had met Orage at a theosophical meeting in London in 1906, when he had jumped up on the stage in the absence of the advertised speaker, to give an impromptu lecture, and shortly after became his lover. She wrote that after about a year 'when Aphrodite had amused herself at our expense, I found a collection of works on sorcery. Up to this time Orage's friend was not Mr Holbrook Jackson, who thought he was, but Mr Aleister Crowley. Well I consigned all the books and Equinoxes and sorcery designs to the dustbin.'"

Crowley's ambition was to restore an ancient wisdom, the Gnosticism that he saw as the original rational attempt at a universal religion that was messed up by Christianity.

As he wrote in *Magick without Tears*:-

> "It appears that the Levant, from Byzantium and Athens to Damascus, Jerusalem, Alexandria and Cairo, was preoccupied with the formulation of this School in a popular religion, beginning in the days of Augustus Caesar. For there are elements of this central idea in the works of the Gnostics, in certain rituals of what Frazer

conveniently calls the Asiatic God, as in the remnants of the Ancient Egyptian cult. The doctrine became abominably corrupted in committee, so to speak, and the result was Christianity, which may be regarded as a White ritual overlaid by a mountainous mass of Black doctrine."[16]

The Romantic movement of Byron and Shelley was a revolt against the principle of unjustified authority, against what Blake called Urizen, (your reason) and in this there were parallels with the ancient Gnostic movement. The Jews were interesting to the ancient world as providing the one alternative to the classical consensus. They were regarded mostly with abhorrence. Gnosticism expresses both this interest and this abhorrence. Many Romantics felt a comparable attraction to the Catholic culture of the south, to precisely the elements which Enlightenment culture ignored, an attraction which is combined with a sternly Protestant repugnance.

As against false Rationalism, the true understanding of Romantic enlightenment means to perceive as many real relationships as possible. Liberation means to be instinctually fulfilled. We may trace a pulse operating through this genealogy of ideas. When a really high point of understanding is reached, it does not rest in itself, but like the God of the Gnostics creates something new, which goes through various emanations until Pistis Sophia (the soul) falls into the prison of darkness and has to escape again, needing help to mount back up to a new position, where the full union of liberation and understanding, real enlightenment, is again possible.

Ideas are not entirely like this, for they are lived by human beings whose personal quests are not limited by some supposed tendency in the movements with which they align themselves. Sometimes, even perhaps often, change comes about from necessarily defensive stances taken against some alien, threatening force. Thus art is forced into a position by the advances of vulgar Rationalism. Vulgar Rationalism is often a child of true reason in that it was originally certain possibilities thrown out by genius which were taken up by other people who gained power thereby. As any enlightenment spreads, its vulgar forms are more easily assimilable and eventually they gain preponderance.

Each successive emanation is farther from the source. Energy dissipates itself, it wishes to discharge. In discharging, it may be diluted for the next generation, and this may continue until it is so far gone into darkness that it is aspired to again. Tension is so low, suggesting Empedocles state of strife, that the movement in that direction can go no further, and a counter movement of love gets going, and eventually the last ditched ideas of the attempted counter reformation, (Iamblichus, Hermes Trismegistus), acquire a dynamic new fascination. Thus creative eras and decadent eras succeed each other throughout history.

At every stage Romanticism has had and continues to have its enemies. Mario Praz quotes the Italian philosopher Croce:-

"This malady (Romantic Decadence) was due not so much to breaking away from a traditional faith, as to the

difficulty of really appropriating to oneself and living
the new faith, which, to be lived and put into action,
demanded courage and a virile attitude, also certain
renunciations of bygone causes of self-satisfaction and
comfort which had now ceased to exist; it demanded
also in order to be understood, discussed and defended,
experience, culture and a trained mind."[17]

This is Hegelian Rationalism, the insinuation that the 'new faith'
can justly demand that we submit ourselves to its authority. In
the recalcitrant material, the refusal to renounce old sources
of satisfaction, lies the real hope of human freedom.

Romanticism is not just the search for the strange and exotic,
it involves the *need* to explore these things. It is related to the
imperialistic impulse. There is a drivenness about it, an inner
imperative, quite the antithesis of a playful dilettantism.

It is noteworthy that people use the Romantic impulse in the
attempt to overcome Romanticism, just as people profoundly
affected by Nietzsche are sometimes led to reject Nietzsche
almost in his own name. In Artsybashev's *Sanine* the
Nietzschean hero throws down his copy of *Zarathustra* in
disgust as too hysterical.[18] John Symonds apparently cultivated
a Crowleyan stare and threatened enemies with his own magical
powers.[19] It is not just the deliverances of reason that
romanticism throws up in its progress, but a titanic urge to
exceed God.

To abandon Romanticism for such a reason is wilful
obscurantism. Always the supposed advance beyond is only

into some new pattern supposedly given by reason that is open to the same kind of objection. I would suggest that Romanticism is actually the core of our distinctive Western civilisation, what Spengler called 'Faustian man'. It is to be found in Protestantism and also in gothic Christianity which in turn derived it from the impact of Islam. I would say Nietzsche is the supreme explicator of this impulse, which we call the will to power. Crowley was its living embodiment.

# Notes

1   Crowley, *Magick Without Tears* p. 447
2   Crowley, *Magick in Theory & Practice* p. xi
3   Crowley, *The Confessions*, p. 114
4   "*Invaluable to all students*" writes Crowley.
5   Brailsford, pp. 213 - 214
6   *History of Western Philosophy* p. 701-710
7   Crowley, *Book of Lies*, p. 172
8   Praz (1930) p. 434
9   Crowley, *Magick in Theory & Practice*, p. 354
10  Crowley, *Collected Works* Vol 1 pp. 224-5
11  Praz (1930) p. 351
12  Regardie (1970) p. 432
13  On such grounds he defends Crowley's blasphemies against Cammell, but draws the line at hunting and other activities which shook his own sensibilities.
14  Crowley, *The Confessions*, p. 216
15  Crowley, *The Confessions*, p. 217
16  Crowley, *Magick Without Tears*, p. 77
17  Praz (1930) pp. xiii - xiv
18  Artzibashef (1914) p. 35
19  *Daily Telegraph* obituary November 2006.

# 2
# Crowley and Protestantism

Another perspective on Crowley's achievement is to view him as the heir and fulfilment of English Protestantism. In his upbringing he experienced some of the worst aspects of that form of religion. Nevertheless Protestantism was the driving force of English history for some centuries and Crowley's anti-Christianity has its roots in some of its impulses. Steeped in English literature and tradition he was happy to recommend such a sternly Protestant work as Bunyan's *Pilgrim's Progress*.

Catholic apologist G K Chesterton famously admonished the young Crowley for his Paganism, writing:-

> "But Mr Crowley is a strong and genuine poet, and we have little doubt that he will work up from his appreciation of the Temple of Osiris to that loftier and wider work of the human imagination, the appreciation of the Brixton chapel."[1]

This was a red rag to Crowley who promptly wrote the satirical poetic drama *Why Jesus Wept* in consequence.

If we nevertheless attempt to follow through Chesterton's suggestion, the first thing we notice about the interior of a non conformist chapel will probably be the prominence given to the pulpit. In this there can be found a certain poetry. We think of the free church preachers thundering from it, wondering at the emotions they inspired and what went on in their minds. If we are used to Anglican or Catholic churches, the non-conformist church is a kind of democratic protest. It has a republican quality and we see how it could thrive in America. There would be feelings of power in the simple doctrines.

In comparison with Anglican and Catholic churches there is something bizarre about the nonconformist chapel. Its very democracy plays fast and loose with immutable tradition, much as Picasso did with the human body. What we think of as religion, or a church interior, is fixed as the shape of the human body is fixed. The strangeness of the free church is that it seems to create democratically a tradition in the way the congregation wants it. It interiorises the Biblical message in the words of the Authorised Version.

But then we recoil when we think too specifically of the preachers and the congregation. The poetry belongs to a part of the mind temporarily distracted from sensual enjoyment.

# Repression

Protestantism is often associated with the so called work ethic and a form of religion which may appear to have nothing whatever to recommend it, being merely justification for an undeveloped soul or personality with an obsession with duty. Such Christianity comes across as a doctrine of self-denial, priggish, hypocritical and morbid. Crowley knew all about this from his teachers and relatives. This life negating character was not just true of outré sects, but included the Anglican mainstream. In the ever popular Christmas carol *Once in Royal David's City* the line:- "*Christian children all must be/ mild obedient good as he*", indicates what sorts of people used to oppress children in England. Against the dourness of Protestant Christianity, even Catholicism itself may pretend to stand for a degree of jollity, and to retain something of the instinct affirmation of the ancient world. Crowley himself, commenting on a verse from *Liber Legis*,[1] once wrote:-

"Catholic Christians are really Pagans at heart; there is usually good stuff in them, particularly in Latin countries. They only need to be instructed in the true meaning of their faith to reject the false veils."

A few years later he corrected himself:-

"An XXI: [1925] After some years spent in Catholic countries, I wish to modify the above. Catholics are dead alike to Spirituality and to Reason, as bad as Protestants."

When Nietzsche and Crowley attack Protestantism, as they both sometimes do, it might be thought that they are targeting the type of the Christian prig, which has undeniably dug itself well into the societies of the Protestant West. It certainly does not exhaust Protestantism. Many other types flourish that might be called Protestant, but that one has been particularly powerful and successful partly because it is so devoted to work.

A gloomy, canting form of Protestantism established itself with the Cromwellian revolution, in the form of Puritan dictatorship. The motives that inspired the Puritan busybodies of the Protectorate are arguably not much different from those that inspired the Ayatollah Khomeini, namely hatred of what is seen as frivolous, decadent distraction, trash culture demoralising youth. What Protestantism became was something miserable as we see in Samuel Butler's *The Way of All Flesh*. That it turned so sour does not alter the fact that for a while it was widely found extremely liberating, especially in England.

The bossy repressive character outlives religious faith. In our secularised Protestant society there is an abundance of so called experts trying to direct people's lives in accordance with their own ideals, teachers, therapists, social workers, sexologists, political ideologues. Society still teems with sanctimonious grotesques, much as it has for centuries. Such figures often express patronising attitudes to the common people, seeing them as in need of the sort of harsh remedies offered by Protestant religion. Without a moral code enjoining restraint, it is said, the people succumb to vice – to drink, drugs, idleness, dissipation. We should look at the values in the minds of the educationists before we accept their claims that what they do is necessary. Ever keen to imprint themselves on the minds of the young, they resemble the religious sects except that they probably have less sympathy and understanding.

Nietzsche once said of the Reformation, from what some might think as an excessively German perspective, that it was a vulgar and plebeian version of the Renaissance. Accordingly he suggested that it would have been a good idea for Luther to have been burned like Huss, thus allowing the Enlightenment to occur 100 years earlier than it did.[5] Science is shallow, he is prepared to admit. Deep feelings belong to religion, which is illusion. He is for science, for Rationalism, Enlightenment. He praises Voltaire. Crowley could not go all the way with this, obviously. He wants some of these feelings and is sympathetic to religion. The man Nietzsche declared his antipode,[6] Richard Wagner, man of deepest feelings, has as prominent a place among the Gnostic saints as Nietzsche himself.

# Directions

As spectacle the Italian Renaissance was of course magnificent, yet it was to a high decree arbitrary and despotic. Protestantism has many different aspects, interpretations and lines of possible development. One line leads back to the Old Testament. However the anti-papal aspect of it can easily relate to the anti-demiurgic, anti-Ialdabaoth perspective of ancient Gnosticism. From one point of view the Protestant project might be seen as the putting an end to Christianity itself, which is a large historical pattern harder to escape than is often thought. This was originally Nietzsche's understanding of Luther. He wanted to finish his work. For most of the time this was Crowley's attitude. He approved the Reformation, and took it very seriously as a historical project.

# & Liberty

There is much tension between the coercive prohibitionist tradition and the popular liberty with which Protestantism is strongly associated. Despite his somewhat tyrannical behaviour as a statesman, Luther is counted a hero in the cause of liberty and so is Cromwell. One root of liberty is the sheer cussedness of an unwillingness to conform, a motive which may also be applied to illiberal purposes.

Luther's distaste for the Neo-Paganism of Rome, cannot be entirely to his discredit. The Rome of his day asked for and demanded dupes. *"Quantum nobis prodest, haec fabula Christi!"*[2] said the man Crowley praised as the best of the atheist Popes. There is much to be said in support of the Protestant revolt against spiritual authority. The Italian pagans of the Renaissance were in some respects innocents. Christianity certainly remained a presence. The full restoration of Paganism was not really on. The revolt against authority was not a revolt against a chimera or a crass misunderstanding. You may choose to live within a framework of certain basic myths and pursue personal ambition within it, or you can try to change that framework, including some of the myths, especially when elements of it clash strikingly with your own will.

Protestant historians have told a stirring tale. Lecky's *History of European Morals from Augustus to Charlemagne* is a compendium of Victorian Protestant prejudices. For modern Europeans, Motley's *The Rise of the Dutch Republic* could be a more inspiring work than Plutarch's *Lives*. Despite what Nietzsche says it can be hard not to see Protestantism as progress. As with Mao Tse Tung in China old values were realised in the fulfiller and destroyer of the old. In the Calvinism of the old style aristocrat William the Silent, freedom of conscience became itself a religious ideal.

The historian Lord Acton (himself a somewhat unorthodox Catholic) traced a key advance in the idea of liberty to the Independents in the English Civil War:-

> "As there was no State Church, there could be no right of coercion over consciences. Persecution was declared to be spiritual murder. The age of Luther and the Reformation was an age of darkness. All sects alike were to be free, and Catholics, Jews, and Turks as well. The Independents fought, as they expressed it, not for their religion, but for liberty of conscience, which is the birthright of man." (*Lectures on Modern History*)

This attitude promoted a kind of individual sovereignty as the fundamental religious value.

There is a conception of the essence of all evil that is Protestant, religious, and sees it as exemplified in phenomena like the Spanish Inquisition. The suggestion that we should tolerate this evil and its expression is one that brings out deep conflicts in society. The so called tolerance promoted by the orthodox Catholic preserves the underlying assumption that his values are the real fundamental ones. His 'tolerance' represents the most basic assault on the essence of Protestant belief. That belief he despises and seeks to colonise.

# Raw will

> "For all its excellence, will Bunyan's ghost haunt the
> forsaken churchyards, and scare the children of the third
> Atheist generation? Why should it, more than *Foxe's Book
> of Martyrs* survive the decay of the virulent Protestantism
> that nourished it with poison?" [3]

There is something very attractive about the old England that
shines through *Foxe's Book of Martyrs*. Filled with the spirit of
this anti authoritarian tract we might want to take the Protestant
martyr for simply the mythological prototype of the dissident.
Out of it we can form a rebellious ideology, which acquires a
national tint and becomes an aspiration to freedom in an older,
simpler sense.

English ideas of freedom are intimately connected with
Protestantism, and are considered to have predated and even
inspired it. Many of the roots of English ideas of freedom lie
in anti-French feeling. Urged on by the modernising enthusiast
Hildebrand, the papally sanctioned Norman Conquest was a
proto crusade. It has been argued that this brought about a
lasting sense of resentment against the papacy among the
English people which was to bear fruit centuries later. Others
trace the Reformation back more aristocratically, among others
to William the Conqueror's refusal to swear fealty to the Pope.
Catholics, on the other hand argue that King John having
surrendered England to Innocent III and only received it back
as a Papal fief, English Protestants are all traitors.

Whether we see it as noble or plebeian, early Protestantism presaged new forms of enjoyment, power and even aristocracy. Protestant Europe has not been always or necessarily socialist and democratic, it has its own forms of authority, its own heroism and adventure. Nietzsche's own anti Christianity is part of that movement. It is noteworthy that Luther was in some ways a Rabelaisian sort of character, much taken with farting. The idea of English liberty which Crowley fully respected, was as much identity as objective ideal. At bottom one embraces it because it is one's own tradition.

Give a bit of mythology to play with and new gods come into being. A god is a creation produced by an enormous concentration of emotion. Protestantism protests, and this was traditionally the heart of the English character. There are hints of liberty even in the coarser aspects of its will to power. Liberty itself has been honoured as a goddess at several times in history. In recent years what we might call the god Yobbo, or the Spirit of Yobbery has been celebrated by such artists as Gilbert and George as the expression of a certain kind of affirmation, freedom itself being the true religious value. Such a character naturally transcends Protestantism and Englishness, as when Crowley conceives himself as the rowdy Irishman who landing in America asks *"is there a government here?"* And being told there is says, *"then I'm agin it."* [4]

Communism, Catholicism and Protestantism, are all radically different perspectives, like different loyalties. Ultimately one is loyal to some particular tyrant, some assertion of naked power.

If the papacy is, in Hobbes phrase *"the ghost of the deceased Roman Empire, sitting crowned upon the grave thereof,"* the English Protestant looks back to certain acts of violence perpetrated by Henry VIII. It is said that Protestant theology only became necessary in England after Henry's reforms to reassure the people who would otherwise feel bereft.

Of course Protestantism, let alone yobbishness, is far from exhausting English identity. There is an underlying civil war in England, symbolised by Catholic versus Protestant. Irreconcilable concepts of evil and therefore what it is worth fighting to the death for and differing concepts of freedom keep up a constant tension. For a while England was the leading Protestant nation in history. Its Protestantism continues to express itself in contemporary atheism, agnosticism and religious indifference. Yet it has lately come about that anti-Catholicism is condemned as bigotry and reviled like anti-semitism. Hatred of the Pope, is a great part of the libertarian tradition. The Catholics see it differently, but it is hardly acceptable that we should misread our history just because of them. Even if the Northern Irish Protestants were as ugly as their enemies allege, their historical cause, their anti-papism, has value in it. It is anticipated that the Irish troubles may eventually resolve themselves as victory for the Republicans brings the disappearance of Protestant cause. Yet this is ultimately a hollow victory as Catholic belief is eroded and English cultural domination becomes ever more pervasive.

# Value of Catholicism

Remove Catholicism far away from its moral and cultural reach, and what is the point of Protestantism? To be fully liberating it requires that catalyst. If Protestantism is to accomplish itself it needs Catholicism with all its evil that it may triumph over it. Without what it was to react against the guiding myths of Protestantism become mere superstition. Put the two in mutual antagonism and we can have an effective escape from the oppression of Christianity itself. Such overcoming is close to the whole purpose, the meaning of life.

> "The brave man rejoices in giving and taking hard knocks, and the brave man is joyous. … He understands that the only joy worth while is the joy of continual victory, and victory itself would become as tame as croquet if it were not spiced by equally continual defeat." [5]

Catholicism has a better survival record than Protestantism. The essential Protestant impulse is forgotten when Catholic and Protestant tolerance are put on the same level. Seventeenth century English Catholicism was heroin and worse. Now Catholics are tolerated, and the Protestant impulse of hatred for presumptions of spiritual authority, is regarded as uncharitable.

Catholic intolerance of Protestantism is worse than vice versa. Protestantism in essence is closer to the ideal of toleration than is Catholicism. For the same reason it is more oppressive for communism to suppress capitalism than vice versa. A spirit of authority is set against a spirit of freedom. The latter may suppress possibilities like Catholicism, to which it feels no inclination. This is oppression, but it is not as bad as the Catholic exaltation of the principle of spiritual authority for its own sake. Yet to those convinced they had the truth the suppression of heresy must have seemed simply like the elimination of alien and tedious nonsense.

## Self-negating decadence

When Protestantism expresses a Hebraic fear of decadence, often what it has in mind is almost identical with Roman Catholicism, with penitence and the cult of the Virgin Mary. In looking back on the past it is easy to underestimate the abhorrence Protestants used to feel for Catholicism. What is Gibbon's decadence but that? We can see why so many of the English decadents become Catholics. The perverse lure of decadence was not for the pride of a Milton's Satan, or the depravity of a Jack the Ripper, but the luxurious self-abasement and moral weakness of the Catholic. This was not really the proud harlot of Babylon but the natural harlot of Spain. Communism, that attracted a later generation, is merely an extreme version of such Christianity.

There are different forms of anti-Christianity. Some hate Christianity because they want to replace it with another religion, like Islam or some secularised form of Judaism. Alternatively one may hate it for Protestant reasons. As the papacy itself came to be seen as an oppression, so does Christian doctrine itself. Anti-clericalism, which is found in Catholic countries, is different from the anti-religious prejudice which is essentially Protestant. If most of us dislike the Pope it is not because we have outgrown all religion, even our Protestantism, rather it is the same impulse that created Protestantism in this country in the sixteenth century. Christianity is found obnoxious for sound English Protestant reasons. It is a matter of conscience.

Frances Yates described the hermetic philosopher Giordano Bruno, burnt as a heretic in 1600 as a Catholic but not a Christian. Likewise it is quite possible even normal, to be a Protestant and protest yourself right out of Christianity. Crowley was working fully in the tradition of the one great period of religious genius in the history of his people. It is the decay of Christianity and consequently of the fully articulated reaction against it, the insidious Catholicisation of modern Protestantism, that puts traditional freedom in such peril. Much Protestantism led into atheism or agnosticism and then the moral force, the energising motive that led it to fight against Papism were lost. So Papism sneaks a surreptitious hold on the unconscious mind.

## French perspectives

The focus is on English history, the English Reformation, because Crowley was English. He claimed to have been French in his previous incarnation as Eliphas Levi Zahed. England and France have grown in symbiosis. Just as the French monarchy arose in resistance to England and English invasion, so ultimately English freedom developed as part of a desire to assert cultural independence and follow a slightly different cultural path. Thus early English Gothic, as at the cathedrals of Wells, Lincoln and Worcester express a healthy and admirable spirit of emulation and good Eris. We can trace English freedom as pre Protestant, pre-Henry VIII, pre-Magna Carta.

In accordance with the dialectic it is helpful to look at a few French views on the subject. Catholic France and Protestant England have produced different takes on intellectual history. Rabelais himself was a product of the Reformation, an ex monk like Luther and hardly to be accounted a Christian. His '*Fay ce que vouldra*' was the very foundation of Thelema.

Pierre Bayle, the herald of the Enlightenment, it is claimed, was not an atheist but his anti-Catholicism struck Frenchmen as anti-Christian. His residual Calvinism led him to attack facile optimists and deists. His defence of toleration was on the basis of conscience. He writes of the obvious immorality of recantation against conscience (for which one should be dammed). His pessimism is characteristic of his age, perhaps, marking a deeper, sounder psychology than the optimism which prevailed later in the eighteenth century. His was the Protestant, Huguenot revenge, stimulating the Eighteenth century enlightenment from Holland.

The historian Taine was very talented but no genius, as evidenced by his portrait of high Victorian English life.[6] Because he favours English Protestantism for reasons of his own, he romanticises it and exaggerates the universality of

Christian belief. He says it is changing, but it is doubtful if it was ever as universal as he says. Much of what he describes survived well into the 1960s in some quarters. He portrays these values, like Thomas Arnold's values, as if they fit. What the son, Matthew, described as philistinism is presented as if it simply expressed the energies of the people.

Taine's journalism hides the repression that Victorian moralism was widely felt to embody. Muscular Christianity was never the feeling of the entire nation. Of course things change and high Victorianism was only a phase. But these phenomena were never taken with the wholehearted commitment he seems to suggest. Taine presents the English as clearly undersexed. He would imply everyone was adjusted to this 'Victorianism' as if only a later generation found it oppressive. So his enthusiasm is partly misplaced. Christianity became the ideology of democratic prejudice, of the values of inferiority and the beliefs of the stupid, popular morality, a collective self-righteous feeling, the idea of the rightness of the common man and popular journalism. Recognising only one side of English Protestantism, Taine conveys the impression that there was at one time no opposition or resentment of this spirit.

The esoteric writer René Guénon shows much arrogance in his assumption of exclusive wisdom, much less wittily carried off than Crowley's. His characterisation of the idiocy of Protestantism exemplifies the French Catholic reaction to the seeming stupidity of the innumerable sects. "*How can truth be so divided?*" it is asked. These may be outer husks but what of it?

What I have called 'Protestant' or 'dissident' method is another way of arriving at truth.

Julien Benda, author of the *Trahison Des Clercs* shows certain ideas clustered together, such as monarchism, hatred of the working class and authoritarianism. This damaged the French monarchist cause just as the Irish problem has damaged both the reputation of the Catholic Irish and the concept of Protestantism as a cause. Benda's concept of the ideal unity of all 'clerks' or intellectuals, as with his admiration of Aquinas lays him open to the criticism of someone like H S Chamberlain, that he supports the essentially authoritarian values of the Latin chaos. He was warning against the alarming tendencies of pre war France, the pre-Vichy syndrome. The best protection against that would be a hatred of oppression that needs to be focussed on some specific cause that is worth rioting about. This is the spirit of Protestant England and it aspires to be universal.

# Decadence

The English Romantics, and even more the English Decadents, recognised that papist culture had something valuable in it and tried to extract some of this value. In the first place, the luxury and corruption that Luther deplored was found attractive as a revival of anti-Christian pagan values. As so often Crowley follows the path pioneered by Nietzsche, with the Decadent even Protestant inspired taste for the Borgias and the consequent suggestion that the Reformation was something to be regretted. Borgia culture was splendid, amoral and apparently pagan. Nietzsche speculated how with Cesare Borgia as Pope, Christianity might have been abolished. Crowley himself says that *"all the best Popes have been atheists."*[15] Pope Alexander VI, another of his previous avatars, was Neo-Pagan but he supported the Inquisition because it brought in revenue. When we admire the Borgias we are not condoning the explicit and stated ideals of a society rather the raw nature which seems to defy those ideals.

It is apparently pagan to treat all ideals as simply vehicles for human energies. Much of what we admire in the Borgias is the defiance of what we understand as Christianity. This seems to be the explanation of the delight we take in them, that they have overcome something we still find oppressive. And might the Renaissance in fact have continued this work abolishing Christianity? Under Leo X the pagan Renaissance produced magnificent art. From the point of view of the visual arts Protestantism must have looked like a serious regression. However the case was different when we consider literature.

# Persecution

Though Protestants were themselves persecutors to some extent, mainstream Protestantism came to involve a visceral revulsion for inquisition and religious persecution. From a rationalistic viewpoint, religious persecution was all in defence of a nothing, superstition, a lie. What value is there in Catholicism that could justify persecution? Yet it is possible to look beyond the illusory hope of a restoration of paganism to find positive value in what was being defended. In Spanish church architecture there is a triumphalist spirit, we can justify it as a common emotion, even a racist feeling. The right to regulate religious belief goes with the freedom of princes, a very aristocratic, by contrast with a bourgeois, freedom. Spanish values include Spanish darkness, well symbolised by the tenebrism of painters like Zurbaran. In what sense are aristocratic values compatible with the darkness of superstition and magic, and how far? It is hard not to feel some affinity for the conquistadors.

Thelema being all about having one's cake and eating it, Crowley would not want to miss out on anything of value in this. He found much value in some Spanish mystics, recommending the *Spiritual Guide of Molinos* as '*a simple manual of Christian mysticism*'.[16] It is one thing to admire the Renaissance papacy for its paganism, but the true decadent wants to experience much more. Bourgeois culture is often treated as a falling off from aristocratic values, with their power fully to satisfy the imagination. The Netherlands conflict was not exclusively a struggle between aristocratic Spain and bourgeois Holland. It was not just the rich bourgeoisie who went for Protestantism, nor did the common people make heroes out of rich merchants. The slightly repellent concept of the bourgeois makes it unhelpful to speak of bourgeois culture as Marx does.

There is a sense in which most moderns are inevitably northern Protestants. We want values to be fully articulated. We have a concept of individual sovereignty. We accept that it is possible to live and gain much pleasure and satisfaction without it. But we could not or certainly should not conceive of dispensing with it in order to do so.

# Luther

"A small minority, including myself, was hot for positive action; definite movements were to be made; in particular, the Mysteries were to be revealed. The majority, especially the Asiatic Masters, refused even to discuss the proposal. They contemptuously abstained from voting, as if to say, "Let the youngsters learn their lesson." My party therefore carried the day and various Masters were appointed to undertake different adventures. Mohammed, Luther, Adam Weishaupt, the man we knew as Christian Rosencreutz, and many servants of science, were thus chosen. Some of these movements have succeeded . . ." [17]

Luther was one of the heroes hymned by the Italian national poet Carducci in his most famous poem *Hymn to Satan*.[18] Luther was no simple revivalist nor St Paul redividus but created something new, and to the believing Catholic diabolical. Protestantism is articulation. It is overcoming on a more than merely personal level. It was a revolt against the Christian scheme insofar as that means spiritual authority. The Republicanism of the Revolution does not abolish spiritual authority as such, its offensiveness has not been felt strongly enough. Escape is possible only on a personal level. It appears that more was needed and that mere Republicanism was inadequate to the task.

Protestant freedom was essentially anti-Catholic feeling in the name of freedom of conscience. It brought a principle of inwardness and multidimensionality. Crowley praises Luther for this, interpreting it as clear progress rather than the obscurantism Nietzsche perversely suggests.

> "There shall be no Property in Human Thought. Let each think as he will concerning the Universe; but let none seek to impose that Thought upon another by any Threat of Penalty in this World or any other World." [19]

It has been pointed out by historians of the period that mere atheism in the early days was inadequate to defeat the Christian structures that were so deeply embedded in the culture. We may see Protestantism as enshrining a myth referring to self-consciousness. It provided dramatic imagery actually expressing this freedom. It suggests a means of reordering society in accordance with the will, instead of merely living in the timeless conservative framework of Catholic tradition. At its best Catholicism offered a freedom based on cynicism, living amid superstition. For the common people it can promote the irresponsibility of the child. The Protestant resents the imputation that he is necessarily repressed and inhibited. Will to power is the thing, the overcoming of resistance, not the release of dammed up energy. In the freedom of the Catholic carnival power is preserved, not really threatened. The flexibility of Protestantism may be seen if for example we treat Christ essentially as a symbol, standing for something like instinctual truth.

# Calvin

"With regard to the question of salvation, by the way, the theory of the exclusive Plymouth Brethren was peculiar, and somewhat trying to a logical mind. They held predestination as rigidly as Calvin, yet this nowise interfered with complete freewill .... There being no authority of any kind, any brother soever might enunciate any doctrine soever at any time, and this anarchy had already resulted, before the opening of our story, in the division of the Brethren into two great sects: the Open and the Exclusive."[20]

Calvin was a great man if a sinister one. He tried to impose his mind upon humanity, reducing Christianity to a more logical if more brutal creed, interesting from the viewpoint of power and ambition. His hard austere vision, exerted a fascination over those of many others. But there is a difference between intelligent people feeling a fascination for such an outlook and being brought up in it, taking it for granted as presuppositions. The vision ceases to be fascinating and becomes narrow repressive and ugly. A fascinating idea can become to a later generation an oppressive monstrosity. Religious beliefs are the debris of history. The excitement of Calvinism initially suggests something like fascism.

# Myth

The religious content of Reformation is best understood primarily as myth. Myth offers a way out of an impasse. As the Greek myths offered a means of understanding certain human realities, the same is true of much of the Biblical material that resurfaced at the Reformation. Thus we can find mythic power, even in such a book as *Foxe's Book of Martyrs*. Immutable tradition has its pressure points, whatever may be said in its favour. It depends upon its police. The ideal of a rational tradition is Protestant. These were the impulses to which Luther and Calvin spoke.

Greek mythology explored the tragic impulse. The urge to tyranny is tragic, because it leads to conflict, with inevitable disastrous consequences. Individual tyranny promises supreme satisfaction. The Emperor Nero was the fulfilment of one strain in classical civilisation. There are of course other ways of looking at life. Spengler had a lot to say about the limitations of classical culture, which he attributed to its lack of an infinite. Certain concepts can deepen or extend the possibility of experience. Mathematical concepts notoriously extend the number of things one can do. Perhaps freedom is such a concept. Crowley was intrigued by C H Hinton's speculations on the fourth dimension, and the idea that freedom might be understood as a four dimensional object progressively manifesting in history.[21] Freedom evolved into sovereignty of conscience. This is its rational formulation, but most of its emotional context can be contained in a pre rationalistic religious form. Individual freedom of conscience is the foundation of the Thelemic doctrine of the true will.

The Pagan Roman Empire was tolerant. With Christianity came a principle of spiritual authority and repression. The plausible quality of early Christianity was based upon what we can now see to be scientific mistakes. The original authority claimed for it was the authority of science, it was an interpretation of the world that purported to be scientifically true. It was persuasive, it had emotional force, apparent history and facts to which it appealed. The moral idea of the virtue of authority was something which crept in later. Protestantism was essentially a reaction against that. It implies that there is something worth caring about.

Pace Marx, the demand for freedom is not just a demand for economic exploitation. It is not 'Jewish' in Marx's sense, but it is in another sense Protestant. Whatever good Marx may want to realise there is another way of valuing which can realise as much good. The hatred of what seems to be socialist tyranny is not basely selfish. It can provide a foundation for everything or almost everything. Whatever good the tyrant offers it offers in a different way. Yet whoever Satan is he is not God's little brother. His grievance is to do with a sense of his privileges having been infringed. There is the sense of a truth that has been curtailed, not a new power that has to be established.

## Modern applications

In our modern society we are instructed to care about some things and not to care about others. The orthodoxies in this sense can seem quite arbitrary even senseless. It seems people happily adapt themselves, even their deeper feelings and concerns to those expected of them by some dominant party in the state. By the standard of what has been identified as the basic impulse of Protestantism this cannot be acceptable. In the absence of a dogmatic church it can seem to be fatuous. The journalist who writes what he does not believe, does not this deserve the name of sin?

Authority in the ancient world was founded upon power or accident of birth. The Catholic church rejected natural power, and set up a putative authority in dogmatic religion. In perceiving the speciousness of the ground the Protestant strikes his own claim to power, proposing an alternative ground, based on a sort of honesty. The pre-Christian set up has returned, newly self-conscious in the face of error. In a world riddled with error and superstition truth puts forward a natural right to rule, something superior to the old pagan right of superior force. Because force is not what is claimed but a specious right.

The power of the Catholic hierarchy is not simply nature and pagan power. Its foundation is lies, deception, superstition. It refutes itself. It is nevertheless a defensible position that to overcome it the Renaissance was not sufficient, that the Reformation was necessary if Christianity was to be undone on a mythic level. Luther was merely the last in a long chain of heretics. The clear perception of the spuriousness of the Catholic claims to authority is potentially an unprecedented liberation of the human spirit. All authority is in fact questioned, in every field. So alternatives present themselves in every case. This is not merely rebellion against authority, which as Nietzsche pointed out, was a feature of the Italian Renaissance.

Where religious feeling still takes a Christian form and colouring, Christian myth and symbolism give the form which religious experience takes. If we examine that experience from a scientific point of view we discover all kinds of natural instincts satisfying themselves in a purportedly Christian format. Protestantism becomes the expression of a demand for power.

In European society there exist different parties, different ideas of the meaning of civilisation. The best of the Protestant tradition is to be seen in terms of a revolt in favour of freedom. Historians point out that it was the princes who started it, not the Emperor who was for so long locked in conflict with the Papacy. One could see it as an anti-Christian movement. But alternatively one could understand it as using all the material of Christianity to express a different impulse. This gives a much clearer concept of the significance of Protestantism and explains why people like Luther begin on the level of myth yet come to have a much wider significance.

# England

England found her historic destiny as the leading Protestant power. The plays of Shakespeare are one expression of her Protestant destiny, the life and work of Aleister Crowley another. She became culturally the leading Protestant nation, whose ideas have been taken over into the US. The significance of Protestantism is related to the development of scientific knowledge, political freedom and the other appurtenances of modern civilisation as we want to give it to humanity. England lost her way in the world, losing the sense of her world mission with her memories of the fires of Smithfield.

Historically English Protestantism includes the seventeenth century Ranters, John Milton, William Blake, and in the twentieth century artists like Stanley Spencer. All these brought sexuality into religion in the sense of the affirmation sex can provide, notably when linked with taboo breaking rebellion. Crowley resonates with this tradition which he grafts onto others from the Orient and from antiquity. Early English Protestantism produced much exotic material of interest to Thelemites.

With Edward Kelly, another of Crowley's avatars, as his skryer, or crystal gazer, Dr John Dee had a number of fascinating conversations with spirits over a period of seven or so years in the 1580s , against a background of personal and political intrigue. Most interesting were their relations with the subversive spirit Madimi, who first appears as a delightful charming child, so endearing Dee that he names his own daughter after her. Later she grows into a sexually provocative adolescent, appearing naked, teaching religious innovation and flagrant immorality, commanding Dee and Kelly to do a wife swap, which they do after overcoming much reluctance from Dee and the horrified reactions of the women. Dee attempts to find theological and philosophical justification for the injunction.

Reading the alchemical writer Thomas Vaughan, we can get more sense of the strength of the idea of Protestant England, the tension that kept England together, with the Protestant sects at one end, keeping up a revolutionary pressure. As for Bunyan, we see why they sent him to prison with attitudes like that, attacking as he did the worldliness of the clergy.

The remarkable antinomian ranter Abiezar Coppe, author of the highly blasphemous *Fiery Flying Roll* of 1649, is one of the flowers of English Protestantism at its most creative. The true understanding of the Hebrew prophetic writing (perhaps the uncensored) lies in learning how to produce its modern equivalent oneself. It is not quite established whether Coppe had an influence on Blake or whether Blake had simply a similar response to scripture. Crowley's *Holy Books* are of course of the same school.

In the twentieth century the Catholic sculptures of Eric Gill express sexualised religion, as with his juxtaposition of the crucified Christ and the naked nymph. From an orthodox Catholic viewpoint this seems heretical. It connects with a strain of English Protestantism, and shows affinities with the painter Stanley Spencer. Of its kind it is perfectly successful, religious erotic art of a quite acceptable kind. Blake, Stanley Spencer, Gill, all bring sex into religion. This is sex as the moment of affirmation. In sex tastes differ. Yet any of us might treat his own sexual tastes as a kind of religious rite, in the service of the nude Goddess.

# Russians

Reading nineteenth century Russian novelists, we learn that the difference between Russian identity and English identity is like a state of being versus a state of struggle. We can try to trace this to religious differences, Orthodoxy versus Protestantism. Protestantism may be seen as a religious form that transcends Christianity. Thus the English may no longer be Christian while remaining Protestant, the essence of Protestantism being protest against a form of authority. The concept of freedom only has meaning in terms of struggle against its antithesis, so the myth has to be constantly renewed. A people guided by a myth of freedom must constantly fight to renew it, it cannot settle into a state of being. Being is precisely what the Russian sought in the people. Karatayev, Pierre's inspiration in *War and Peace*, is just a silly old peasant, mild, resigned, religious.

Dostoyevsky disapprovingly quotes the poet Sidney Dobell as saying that for all its many shortcomings Protestantism will survive because it is 'educational'.[22] Dobell characterised Protestantism as a *"wrangling club of half-thinking pedants, half-taught geniuses and untaught egotists of every type"*. The half-taught geniuses are men like Boehme, Blake, Bunyan. But there are well taught geniuses like Milton, Calvin, Hooker. Protestantism was a phase in the emancipation of religious experience.

# Morals

The Protestant urge for freedom takes the form of a moral impulse based on its own conception of truth. Its opponents see it as wickedness and blasphemy, miserable crime. The person whose belief it is has no right to a hearing, no right to liberty or even life. The defiance of accepted doctrine is defiance of what conceived itself as virtue and spiritual truth.

If Protestantism represents something objectively significant, it may seem paradoxical that it can come out of the system of lies and errors that is original Christianity. One alternative is to think of the latter not so much as lies, but differently as something neither true nor false, mere framework, a kind of creative despotism, nothing to do with morality. Truth is a value that emerges from competition, from resistance to despotism. God Himself might even be redefined in this way.

The most fundamental offence against freedom is the prohibitionist idea that it is possible to lay down a pattern of happiness to which we have a right to expect everybody to adapt. Such freedom would be such a basic right that it is irrelevant if it comes with some disadvantages from a Utilitarian viewpoint. We could think of it as the heart and essence of Protestant identity which we should preserve at all costs. Some societies express an odious prohibitionist principle as the very foundation upon which everything is based. Such can be the case in societies where Protestant rebellion has made no impact and alternatives like 'Asian values' have credibility. Where there is a true spirit of freedom it is rooted in rebellious tradition, rather than rationalistic ideas.

The Protestant struggle is essentially the struggle to make your own religion. In Catholicism spiritual authority derives from the church hierarchy, ultimately from the Pope. Erastianism puts it in the hands of the secular authorities. With Presbyterianism it is democratised in the hands of church elders. The idea of early Protestantism was that spiritual authority was written down in the *Bible*. This authority was used against the hierarchy. A natural step further was to subordinate this authority to the 'Inner Light' as the Quakers did. As in Protestantism the Pope became the Antichrist, so in the tradition of western Christendom Christian doctrine itself became identified as anti life. It became the one great iniquity under the new form taken by the spiritual quest.

Crowley's image appeals on a universal religious level. His appeal genuinely breaks through all barriers of intellectual elitism. Though anti-elitism may often express a conscious democratising and Ialdabaoth mentality there are times and places where such barriers become irrelevant. One relates to people through what one desires of them. One may desire without patronising.

> "At the Reformation, we find a nugatory attempt to remove the Black element. The Protestant thinkers did their best to get rid of the idea of sin, but it was soon seen that the effort could only lead to antinomianism; and they recognized that this would infallibly destroy

the religious idea as such."[23]

It can be foolish simply to lash out and destroy something one has reason to hate. Affirmation takes many forms always surmounting new obstacles. For one generation to want to communicate its experience to another, a certain amount of bad needs to be transmitted. Christianity can seem a kind of abscess, draining poison from far afield. To hate it is an emotion that can be highly productive. Simply to eliminate it is hardly an adequate or progressive response, it creates no dialogue. Blasphemy can be one form of genuine religion.

Historians write of the books in the average English household in the early eighteenth century. Almost universal were Bunyan and *Paradise Lost*. This could bear out what was said about Protestantism educating. Milton could be profoundly educative in some one sense, going far deeper than the Bible into fundamental Christian Mysteries. J C Powys said that much evangelical Protestantism was based not on the Bible but on *Paradise Lost*.[24] There is sublimity here. But with respect to the Bible, sublimity is what remains of the authority that has been taken away.

> "After all, Milton was a great poet; and the subconscious artistic self of him was therefore bitterly antagonistic to Christianity. Not only is Satan the hero, but the triumphant hero. God's threats have not 'come off'. It is the forces of evil, so called, that manifest in strength and beauty of form. The glories of the saints are tinsel."[25]

From Milton came Blake and from him it is but a few short steps to Aiwass. We may see the law of Thelema as a development of basic Protestantism. Luther said *"Here I stand I can do no other,"* Crowley *"Thou has no right but to do thy will."*[26] We may speak of a man following his conscience or of his following his true will. What is 'my God', but my innermost satisfaction? To pursue that can be construed as the supreme virtue even as leading to saintliness, whereas the pursuit of one's 'own will' is vulgarly regarded as the height of evil. Where is the difference? Perhaps that the one who uses the God idiom is expected to be afflicted with inhibition.

The God of the Old Testament was a racial, nationalistic God. What was godly was what served the nation. Few scruples stood in the way of this end. God stood for the collective will, the morality needed to bind a people together. Protestantism substitutes individual for collective will.

In the eighteenth century, Mandeville wrote of the principle that that no man be coerced against his conscience as essential to a free society. The authoritarian may cynically deride such a principle. For the Catholic concept of heresy deviation from an official line is inherently sinful or criminal. The Protestant idea that freedom and sovereignty of conscience are really central is not taken head on. The Catholic reserves the fight to suppress heresy, though he may tolerantly refrain from using it. It is self-evident to him that there are values more important than freedom, that freedom is only a luxury that needs to be put in its place. To the Protestant, sovereignty of conscience is the source of all values, for the Catholic the source is derived from outside. He is happy to submit to a principle of authority. Submission to authority is natural and good to him.

The Catholic opposition refuses to understand the Protestant case for freedom, and fails to recognise its own authoritarianism as tyranny. Scepticism is a form of relativism on which the Catholic case depends, and was much exploited by the Jesuits. One of their arguments is that dogmas are much like rules of grammar and language, and that to insist they be changed for some ideal of freedom is absurd, vulgarly personal ambition. There is an idea of religion which sees it primarily as esoterism. The view of religion primarily as morality is a product of our own rebellious Protestant spirit. The coercive aspect is something we resist. And we want the whole of history and nature to be covered by our scientific principle, we don't want to spare any bit for miracle.

Protestant culture itself is a form of resistance. It promotes cultural forms which are self-subsisting, detached from any need to belong to a grand synthesis. All the time Catholicism struggles for supremacy hoping for the extirpation of Protestantism. The priestly motive attacks the self-subsistent. How can the priest be resisted unless there is a good motive for hating him? And how can one hate what is simply religiously tolerated?

# Wesley

By the middle of the eighteenth century English Protestantism
had developed into a prejudice for liberty that was anarchic in
character. Smollet paints a fascinating picture of 1760s England
in *Humphrey Clinker*. The gentleman Bramble deplores the
mixing of the social classes and speaks about the abuse of the
ideals of liberty and the Protestant religion. There is the idea
of the 'patriot', presumably some kind of Wilkite,[27] Protestant,
liberty obsessed, proto imperialist. The servant Clinker, falsely
imprisoned for theft, reveals himself as a Methodist preacher
disturbing the turnkey who would prefer his charges to 'die
like true born Englishmen' rather than 'canting weavers'. After
1760, Christianity became more of a curse as morality and
manners began to change. Before Victoria came to the throne
a sabbatarian gloom had descended over much English life. It
seems the Methodist movement played a large part in bringing
this about.[28] Eighteenth century England was a place of energy
and vigour, where worry about demoralisation seems somehow
irrelevant. Though the threat of the mob was still something
strong and feared, the democratic threat was not the same thing
that it later became. It did not mean quite the same depressing
demoralisation. There is much about the brutality of Georgian
England that upsets us, with its hangings. Yet, perhaps the worst
part of this is an oversensitivity to it.

The Wesleyan Christianity which overran the country and
indirectly much of the Protestant world originated in Oxford,
the most Christian city in the Kingdom according to Thomas

Hardy, the place from where Richard Dawkins currently proclaims his simple gospel of atheistic materialism. Wesleyism was a reaction against paganism, not against popery. It was the Christianity that was introduced, with its tremendous encouragement to the over sensitivity of the female and ignorant that made nineteenth century English Protestantism such a poisonous brew. If eighteenth century culture was like a reliving of the Italian Renaissance, Wesley was its Savonarola or St Paul. Once again we see an admirable Pagan culture falling to evangelical fanaticism.

> "We have, however, examples plentiful enough of religions deriving almost exclusively from the Black tradition in the different stages. We have already mentioned the Evangelical cults with their ferocious devil-god who creates mankind for the pleasure of damning it and forcing it to crawl before him, while he yells with drunken glee over the agony of his only son."[29]

# Conclusion

The disharmony of morality with the will means that morality is experienced as a coercive pressure. Against morality is evil, the Devil. Identify the coercive element in all that is expected, what is desired of you, what women desire of you. There is the idea that one should think and feel other than as one does think and feel. All these coercive factors should be made explicit. Thus what is demanded of you may be easier to resist.

With the Protestant freedom impulse, there are internal contradictions. The intolerance (of Catholicism) creates what eventually may seem a superior more powerful and free position. In England this led to religious indifference. Scotland took a different route. First was the mission to rid civilisation of superstition, and then after that, comes Romanticism. 'No Popery' is a fight to clear the state of a present danger. What no longer threatens may be romantically enjoyed.

Protestantism suggests emancipation from gregarious values. For all its intense moral seriousness it contained different strands and went in different directions. It is sometimes argued that the Latin temperament is in some ways less free than the Northern, because it tends due to a greater gregariousness to adhere more faithfully to publicly accepted values. There is more of a participation in a public culture, and less obstinate eccentricity of tastes and values. Protestantism was a movement from below, associated with individualism stimulated by the reading of the Bible. It was a movement to individual self-sufficiency, and in that respect asocial.

Thelemic morality is self-assertion, as against the inhibition and restraint which are the Christian norm. *The only sin is restriction.* This is the level on which we need to deconstruct Christianity, and honour the Borgias, while being prepared to acknowledge William the Silent as a hero in the mould of Achilles. Aristocratic values involve fighting for what one believes in, or at least fighting. We champion whatever values we happen to believe in, against Spain and the Inquisition.

Sometimes history is so well known as to become a trap. England was at its most free when it most abhorred the spirit of the Inquisition. Although in one sense the Reformation may seem to have been successful in that explicitly Christian belief has now almost died out, in another it might seem to be on the verge of defeat. The resistance to conformism of thought may seem to have lost much of its ground, and we see the return of centralised doctrine, no longer explicitly Christian, but demanding our obeisance in a coercive manner. Puritan bossiness combines with an un-Protestant contempt for freedom of conscience. If we again become slaves to the zeitgeist the Reformation will have been successfully reversed. The master morality of Thelema is a significant bastion of resistance to such a deplorable outcome.

# Notes

1  Crowley, *Collected Works*, p. 203
2  "Mercy let be off: damn them who pity! Kill and torture; spare not; be upon them!"
3  Crowley, *The Law Is For All*, p. 275
4  *Ibid*
5  Nietzsche, *Human all To Human*, p 147
6  *Portable Nietzsche* p. 662
7  "How much we profit from this fable of Christ!"
8  Acton (1960) p. 193
9  *The Magical Record of the Beast 666*, p. 215
10  80
    {Kappa-Epsilon-Phi-Alpha-Lambda-Eta Pi}
    BLACKTHORN
    The price of existence is eternal warfare.
    Speaking as an Irishman, I prefer to say: The price

of eternal warfare is existence.
And melancholy as existence is, the price is well
worth paying.
Is there is a Government? then I'm agin it! To Hell
with the bloody English!
"O FRATER PERDURABO, how unworthy are these
sentiments!"
"D'ye want a clip on the jaw?" p. 70

11   Hobbes, Leviathan ch 47

12   From *Magick without Tears* p. 78

13   Yates (1964) p. 351

14   Taine (1870) *Notes on England*

15   Crowley, *The Book of Lies*, p. 101

16   Crowley, *Magick in Theory & Practice*, p. 210

17   Crowley, *The Confessions*

18   Gittò la tonaca
Martin Lutero;
gitta i tuoi vincoli,
uman pensiero,

19   Crowley, *Liber Aleph* p. 35

20   Crowley, *The Confessions*, p. 41

21   Crowley, Moonchild, p. 63

22   Dobell, *Diary of a Writer* p. 264

23   Crowley, *Magick without Tears*, p. 81

24   Powys (1915) p. 75

25   Crowley, *The Confessions*, p. 81

26   *Liber Al* I 42

27   A follower of John Wilkes

28   Smollet's *History of England*, vol. xv., pp. 121, 122:
"Imposture and fanaticism still hang upon the skirts of
religion. Weak minds were seduced by the delusions of
a superstition, styled Methodism, raised upon the
affectation of superior sanctity, and pretensions to
divine illumination. Many thousands were infected with
this enthusiasm by the endeavours of a few obscure

preachers, such as Whitefield, and the two Wesleys, who found means to lay the whole kingdom under contribution."

29   Crowley, *Magick without Tears*, pp. 75-76

# 3
# Aleister Crowley and Philosophy

The reading list Crowley provides in *Magick in Theory and Practice* includes heavyweight works of philosophy like Erdmann's *History of Philosophy*, the *Essays* of David Hume, Berkeley's *Dialogues*, and Kant's *Prolegomena to any Future Metaphysics*.[1] Elsewhere he commends Bertrand Russell's notoriously difficult *Principia Mathematica* which he says everyone should read.[2] In addition are classic works of oriental philosophy, such as *The Questions of King Milinda* and the *Upanishads*.

Crowley is not writing as a philosopher, and his thoughts on philosophy might be considered subordinate to his interests in Magick and Kabbalah. Both of these involve the idea of the limitations of philosophy, and the need to pass beyond it. Nevertheless some serious philosophy is an important aspect of his teaching. There are vast riches in the history of philosophy, most of which is simply and easily forgotten. Charismatic mystics like Crowley manage to recover some of this and keep it alive, helping to open up almost limitless worlds. Beyond that however, his whole career and personality raise some pressing philosophical questions on their own account, to do with the nature of genius and ambition.

In writing as he does Crowley cannot avoid the expression of philosophical opinions. He uses philosophy for purposes that may seem different from the professional philosopher's concern with logical argument. Nevertheless he runs into philosophical problems which find expression as spiritual states. Spiritual crises express themselves as philosophical perplexity and vice versa.

In Crowley's thinking we can identify much Nietzsche and a certain amount of Hegel. When he was a student at Cambridge, Hegel inspired Absolute Idealism was in vogue. Some things he says presuppose that. Some of his pronouncements are just up to date philosophy, rather than the mystical illumination casual readers may take them for. He was concerned to keep abreast of contemporary thinking, if only to counter whatever challenge might be presented to his own programmes.

Nietzsche has been praised for his incomparable capacity to generate thought,[3] which suggests the possibility of moving beyond him into other possible ideas, even opposite ones. The young Crowley was far from isolated in his Nietzscheanism. As Arthur Symons wrote in 1907:-

> "Thought today, wherever it is most individual, owes either force or direction to Nietzsche, and this we see on our topmost tower, the Philistine armed and winged, without the love or fear of God or man in his heart, doing battle in Nietzsche's name against the ideas of Nietzsche. No one can think and escape Nietzsche."[4]

Studying Nietzsche we see how some fragment ripped out of context and interpreted slightly obliquely may still be stimulating in the extreme. This is very like the way people used to read the *Bible*. We understand how Bible reading could lead to a sort of emotional debauchery for certain sorts of people.

We can trace the philosophical and logical steps which drove Crowley to uphold the *Book of the Law* as the centre of his message. There is a philosophical framework to that work and it is essentially Nietzsche. To stick with this does not appear to have been his original intention. He hints that he wants to go beyond, into some sort of Kabbalah, where opposite ideas balance each other out. There is a natural desire to question and negate, to free from the constraints of any belief whatever. However, it ultimately becomes clear that if you completely dispense with a structure of belief you end up in self destructive paradox. At various points Crowley clearly states his belief in the bankruptcy of rational thought, its failure to bring certainty.[5] If this is taken as a statement within philosophy it is open to all sorts of objections. It may however be understood differently.

Before his commitment to Thelemism came the teaching hailed by Fuller in *The Star in the West*.[6] Crowley's early poetry contains much philosophy[7] on the basis of which Fuller feels able to assert, among much else, that "the philosophical principles of Berkeley and Hume combined form what may be known as the philosophical theme of Crowleyanity".[8] This pre-Thelemite

Crowleyanity did not meet with the success that was hoped for it.

The intensity of Crowley's intellectual ambition runs him into some characteristic philosophers' dilemmas. We may grant that the philosopher begins with a generous impulse. In the words of the *I Ching:- "(It is as if it were said), 'I have a cup of good spirits,' (and the response were), 'I will partake of it with you.'* ".[9] This would be Fuller's 'New Wine' of Crowleyanity. The philosophy he advocates is meant as a social and cultural improvement, a liberating reform. It feels like benevolence, and there is no particular reason to doubt that it is. Encountering indifference, however, and confronting putative alternatives, it easily comes about that it turns into the defensive demand to define the paths to enlightenment, which is to say a selfish ambition. The passion to spread enlightenment becomes the desire for the status of a Buddha or bodhisattva. Such a philosopher encounters frustration when his message is ignored or rejected. The liberator threatens to become the tyrant. These are the cycles presented in William Blake's *Prophetic Books*.

His negation may involve rejection of all joy that is associated with the rejected ideas. Soon this philosophy becomes involved in a very personal problem which demands a particular solution. This is the sort of crisis Crowley identified with the horrors of the Abyss. True to the name he adopted at initiation, Perdurabo, "*I will endure unto the end*," he defiantly persists with his own will and ambition. The main object comes to be to reject the alien hostile judgement which has to be shown to rest upon a lie.

For a solution he has to return to the essentially Nietzschean philosophy that underlies the *Book of the Law*. So rather than offering a new, or even an old philosophy in its own right, an alternative to Nietzsche, Crowley's Kabbalism is to rest on the clear philosophical foundation of that book and all his Kabbalistic thinking comes to be based around the philosophical framework contained therein, and cannot seriously deviate from it. Though the huge ambition for revolutionary reform fail completely, there is energy, originality and potential wisdom in it. Once across the Abyss, much may be salvaged.

## Kabbalah

Kabbalah is like a practical combination of Neo-Platonism and Gnosticism. Apparently it was strongly influenced by the early mediaeval philosophy of John Scotus Erigena.[10] It needs a lot of study for this extraordinary system to impress itself on the mind and be appreciated at its true worth.

As Gershom Scholem points out, the Kabbalah introduces myth, which seems on the face of it very anti-Judaic, into the heart of Judaism. Leaving aside the possibility of anything supernatural, it promotes a philosophy of life that is magical and egoistic. It is a philosophy that makes desire paramount, and can therefore liberate from slavish views. Naturally enough, Scholem writes contemptuously of Crowley's understanding of Kabbalah.[11] An orthodox Jew may be able to swallow the idea of a Christian Kabbalah, but Crowley's mockery is hardly tolerable.

One aim of the Crowleyan Kabbalah is to capture the intoxication of creative thought, as known to the solitary genius. The idea is that beyond any truth, any one-sided philosophy, lies something like a map of all possible ideas. The combinations of the sephiroth are allegedly comprehensive enough to cover everything. The creative enjoyment that can redeem life must be of an intensity that transcends everyday enjoyment. Kabbalah has its roots in ecstatic experiences.

Hegel expressed a comparable hope of complete understanding. Some people who want to get away from Nietzsche are drawn instead to Hegel. Even if the main thrust of Hegel's philosophy is currently unacceptable, many still find him modern and relevant. He claims to have given a complete logical and historical survey of all the forms of thought. In the obscurity of Hegel there is something resembling a mystical idea that there is something to be understood at the very centre. Along the way there are flashes of understanding through all the sketches of the general form of ideas, as if Hegel had already thought everything. He gives an impression of all knowingness. The Kabbalah does this too. To understand Hegel is to see how he can seem to be entirely right; it is to see the desire he appeals to, the motive, to see Boehme and the Kabbalah in him.

It can appear very difficult to summarise or explain Crowley's central idea. Stated boldly much of it may sound like outrageous ungrounded assertion. Perhaps what is most important in, for example, the idea we are entering the age of Horus is the underlying claim of the freedom to think and feel in such ways. Much of Crowley's work is a kind of lyrical intoxication. The underlying ideas are presupposed, and are very largely Nietzschean. He plays variations on certain Nietzschean themes. In his appeals to mystic, incomprehensible authority, the object is not to bind and subjugate. He is reliving modes of experience from various corners of history. There is a difference between the ecstatic freedom of the mystic and the depressing thraldom of superstition.

The more successful a religion or ideology becomes the more it will absorb the whole framework of debate, so that all differences of opinion are to be discovered within its symbolic framework. Thus those people who oppose its predominant and original tendency will, rather than rejecting the religion, sophisticate and deepen it. No doubt given a certain training it would have been possible for even a great heretic to curtail his heretical impulse and keep his ideas within the bounds of some orthodoxy. But sometimes the will to heresy is the will to life, whereas orthodoxy is just death.

Instead of the Hebrew or Christian scriptures Crowley works on his own writings. *Liber Legis* lends itself to Kabbalistic analysis just as well as other scriptures. The real lesson is that each of us can work on our own.[12] One may look at Kabbalah as a journey around what one knows. It is a way of inducing peculiar states of mind, that are useful and/or desirable, reinvesting in all the knowledge one has, or has had. Some of the excitement people can get now from computers is comparable to what people used to get from Kabbalah. Lull's art is a similar thing.

Kabbalism involves infusing words and letters with power, and techniques of jumping from idea to idea with the object of inducing a certain mental state to which special concepts apply, a form of lucid intoxication such as occurs with certain drugs. Essentially it is a strengthening trip around what one knows, yet is likely to forget.

For opening up all the delightful possibilities open to the mind, all this possible treasure, there are classifications based on philosophical assumptions, but the least loaded are indexes based simply on language, and ultimately upon letters and numbers. Kabbalah as Crowley describes it provides a symbolism for handling the entire range of possible thoughts and ideas, allied to the decimal system. (The binary system is represented by the *I Ching*.) It is a shorthand, not a means of discovering what is wrong or right and not a substitute for experience. It is meant as a way of classifying all the ideas one has, or the world of ideas in which one moves, in that case from holy scripture. All sorts of ideas are stimulated in the memory from mere words. There are states of mind one can get to by following associations, forming patterns in a form of intellectual dance. The Kabbalistic scholar starts studying one thing, one combination. He makes discoveries. Then his illumination spreads to surrounding areas as he gradually gains the insights he desires.

Rejecting the concepts that others live by may be deliberately shutting yourself off from joy. By the Kabbalah we may raise ourselves out of this damned condition, to recover our right reason, and this means we must find a set of concepts that are adequate to what we demand of them. Then we become capable of great tasks. We discover the values of the letters of the English alphabet. We enter states of mind that bring creative inspiration. Thus Kabbalah inspired John Dee, the great magus, inspirer of the Elizabethan Renaissance and of English imperialism.

Kabbalah involves mystical commentary on dogmas. Dogmas suggest restraint, constraint, repression, but the mystical is a way round that. And in the Kabbalah there is sound psychology, some almost Freudian suggestions of the place of sexuality in life, as with Yesod, the foundation, the pillar, the lower righteousness, the phallus.

An especially noteworthy example of Crowley's Kabbalistic working is the *Book Of Lies*, which he justly acknowledged to be one of the best things he had written. It consists of 93 chapters with the 'subject of each chapter determined by the qabalistic import of its number.'[13] This is like a journey round Crowley's mature mind, his preoccupations and most exalted ambitions.

## Magick

If Kabbalah is one candidate for something beyond philosophy, magick is another. For Crowley, Magic(k) is all to do with will.

In Sir James Frazer's *Golden Bough*, still an excellent introduction to the subject, will is the original keynote of Magic. Unfortunately this view has recently become controversial.

Frazerian accounts of Magick and ritual had an extensive literary influence in the twentieth century. He has come under sustained attack in recent years, together with some of the dichotomies like the magician/witch, magic/religion, or traditional archetypes like magical secrecy. It is said that social science has moved on from the era of Frazer and Budge. Scholarship itself, however, may sometimes conceal a philosophical or ideological agenda. In some quarters there is intense opposition to the attempt to uncover universal patterns of thought, which seems to be at the heart of Edmund Leach's objections to Frazer and Mircea Eliade.[14]

Mogg Morgan has pointed out that it was noticed long ago that Egyptian religion was so suffused in Magick that in that case the distinction cannot clearly be made. He writes truly enough:-

> "Egyptian magic cannot be opposed to religion and the western dichotomy of 'religion vs. magic' is thus inappropriate when describing Egyptian practice."[15]

He quotes Sir Alan Gardiner (1915):-

> "That magic should have been regarded as an attribute of a deity and a fortiori as itself a deity destroys at one blow the theories of those who discern a fundamental distinction between what is religion and what is magical."

That appears to go too far. There is a useful distinction that is not so easily destroyed, however blurred it might sometimes be.

I have no concern to promote Frazer as anthropologist, but he was a creative thinker and, together with Wallis Budge, a significant influence on Crowley, as modern anthropology obviously could not be. Crowley's Magick was to a great extent rooted in these ideas, and they do have a clear logic of their own. While the religion/Magick dichotomy may not be based on first hand field research, it is a useful distinction for thought. Critics may call it a dogma, I would rather call it an elucidatory concept. With such principles nineteenth century western rationalism meets the rest of the world. It is anyway vital to Crowley's idea of Magick, and to obliterate it is to move away from him and his ideas. If Crowley's Magick, indeed his whole way of thinking is to be upheld, it has to be defended against modern tendencies to deconstruct it.

In *The Golden Bough* magic appears as primitive science, the effort to achieve the object of the will by bypassing the known laws of nature. In this sense magic is the attempt to produce an effect by pseudo causation, which is to say the connection between the cause and the effect is in a sense arbitrary. Magic may include a formal ritualised method of bringing about some state of mind. The connection between the ritual and the desired state is not unalterable, absolute or fixed in nature. Much art and culture may be thought of as systems of magic. The zeitgeist itself is a magical aura or framework. The concept of magic elaborated by Frazer, following original suggestions by E B Tylor, is an admirable tool of analysis.

It can be used to classify ideas like psychoanalysis, that are interesting but not to be taken as scientifically true. It also has application to politics. Most programmes to overcome decadence have a magical character. That is to say there is an objective and action that is supposed to procure it, via the mediation of something supposedly resembling natural laws. Frazerian magic is about achieving the objectives of the will. Thus there is right wing magic and left wing magic. Communism and fascism each involve much magic. It may be felt you cannot have any kind of freedom until you have removed the immediate threat, the thing that is throttling you. Leninism may be considered magic of the blackest kind. To end up feeling good and secure, you have to murder and destroy in the most extreme way.

Modern western society is pervaded by the theories of Marx and Freud. Essentially these are magic, this is the ground of their appeal. So the theory of magic outlined by Frazer is more fundamental than they are. Whatever its faults, he attempted something which gets priorities in the right order. From this point of view what is most interesting about Marx and Freud is what makes them so seductive given that we cannot accept they are true.[16] They are supposed to be deep and intellectual and they promise interesting results. Some form of mental boost is acquired by accepting these ideas.

The Malinowski theory of magic is more patronising than the Tylor-Frazer. Magic may serve the function of arousing useful emotion, but every ritual needs justification. To admit one's own arbitrariness is to get demoralised and die.

Public magic is one thing, perhaps more typically the magician operates on his own, serving his own individual ends. Often the objects of desire are more internal than external. Magic can serve individual desire, as a system, artistic and philosophical, designed to secure satisfaction in a largely frustrating milieu and society. Systematic use of magical technique is a refinement and systematisation of egoism. Such a magician is a form of egoistic philosopher who makes of his personality and his philosophy a dramatic work of art.

Magic, though looking primitive, suggests a deeper penetration of the cosmos than any rational philosophical doctrine. Some primitive peoples appear delightfully free of some of our most immovable taboos.[17] The most malevolent and destructive impulses may be allowed free scope without great harm ensuing and without much sense of guilt. A race of sorcerers one can warm to, while a race of murderers might not be so appealing.

Magick carries such moral detachment into more advanced civilisation. It becomes literate and intellectual. More interesting than the often sordid magic of the mediaeval grimoires, is the way in which more sophisticated forms of magic bypass the limitations of doctrine and dogma to the same end of fulfilment of the will. The magician is not bound by any particular doctrine of life, which is at best merely an instrument. He breaks through and exploits the weak points in any doctrine. Hence comes the inexplicable nature of much that he does, and also its subversive quality. The renunciations of magical oaths are not, as is naturally imagined, moral taboos or even laws of hygiene, they merely express the facts of magical working. The magician does forgo a certain kind of security and certain kinds of satisfaction. The orthodox routes to the orthodox goals of life are barred him. This is principally because he refuses to abase himself, to commit himself thoroughly to the values of his day. He cannot invest all his energy in some orthodox career, because the rewards seem paltry to him.

As for the accusation that he sells his soul to the Devil, this is almost the converse of the truth. It is the conforming majority who sell their souls, he is the one who most steadfastly refuses to do so. Therefore he is unable to enjoy some of the pleasures that the majority enjoy. To commit yourself to a scale of values is not merely to permit yourself to be judged according to those values but to open yourself to enjoy the good they promise. The slave flourishes in the approval of his master. One is playing a recognised game, with recognised rules and is therefore open to successes and failures within the context of that game. One of the most obvious preconditions of success is that the game be played wholeheartedly, for you are in competition with others who have committed their whole selves to the game.

Marlowe's Dr Faustus is not a magician at all, but is a precise parable of the ordinary ambitious man. Goethe's *Faust* is not an esoteric parable but an attempt to replace Christianity by humanism. Faust is not a mage, he is everyman. He is looked over by a benevolent deity who gives him permission to do what he does. He is not even aware of the deity. This is outright theism. Goethe is inventing a new conception of God, albeit a more humane one than had existed hitherto, he is creating values for future society, a future culture. This presages and parallels Hegel.

We might well want to say that magic is superior to religion even though Frazer thought religion was superior.[18] For a long time Christianity offered the most powerful magic in the world. For a while this set of symbols had immense power whatever the motive behind their original creation. Christianity became a form of paganism, for a while not so much a faith as a mechanism for manipulating the universe. Christian myth was a symbolism of natural forces. Magical Christianity was a cover for exploring everything, with the emphasis on the exploration not the Christianity. One could take the Pauline epistles on the level of scientific documents. The real motive, however, was the satisfaction of the will in the form of an infinite curiosity.[19]

The ideal of rational magic is to gain access to all the treasure of the past by specific acts of the will. This magical and Neo-Platonic aim differs from the all encompassing systematised emotion of the Hegelian, which is monotheistic by comparison. For the magician there is no great concern about the Absolute, or the objective of which all other objectives are a part. There can be some quite specific and limited objectives.

Today we can move back much further than the Bible in the study of our civilisation's origins, right to Sumerian myths and their magic. The Golden Dawn helped to bring much older religious forms back into western consciousness. The Pagan magician believes in sheer exercise of the will as a means of attaining happiness. That is different from having no religion, which suggests mere pursuit of inclination. The advance in rational control comes with return perhaps to something once known and since lost as was the magic of the Egyptians.

We like to think of Egyptian civilisation as having had a close understanding of the Great Work and what the real point of life is, notably the sexual nature of it, that is remote from the understanding of the adolescent Buddhist. This is coming to terms with oneself and all one's experience. One transmutes what is painful and unsatisfactory, meaning everything that is against the Great Work, that is to say against the alchemical transmutation of one's own life. We think of Egypt as a culture where such wisdom was encouraged.

Magic can have the same revitalising force as religion. Egyptian magic involves an ideal of sexual integration different from the democratic ideal that is promoted in modern western society. It has been suggested that Wallis Budge, Egyptologist, used to assist Florence Farr,[20] and was sympathetic to the Egyptianism of the Golden Dawn, possibly closer to a genuine sympathy with the old Egyptian civilisation than anything for thousands of years.

Crowley made use of the Ancient Egyptian, the first grandly systematic religion, to convey the idea of a progression of aeons. The occultist may tend to uphold the ideal of the Renaissance mage and despise popular religion. Yet if it is part of one's task to restore paganism one will endeavour to manipulate popular superstitions rather than merely despising them.

We can follow how Neo-Platonic philosophy became Christian philosophy, looking at it from the magician's point of view. Dogmatic belief opens up new experiences, so we try dogmatic belief. There is a point of view from which the distinction between faith and doubt vanishes. Salvador Dali maintained that Christian faith is like surrealism. He intensely admired the Christianity of Rome from a visual and architectural point of view. Insofar as faith desires this, it is triumphalist. But we should not be misled by the Blavatskyan or Rosicrucian myth of hidden Masters or Adepts into thinking of history as entirely rational.

Magical experience flourished at the Renaissance, an age when the wisdom was revered and the latent energies of man could find expression. 'As above so below', meant that correspondences operate through all fields of human experience. The Renaissance culture of magic contrasts with the modern obsession with specialisation. Rather than separate fragmented wisdoms, then the whole wisdom would be brought into the pursuit of a specialised task. The eternal was brought down into the particular.

There is a suggestion that there is in the magical civilisation of the past a deeper, more abiding form of satisfaction than anything our modern age has been able to throw up. Against this Marshall Mcluhan famously objected that modern art has been precisely concerned with resurrecting primitive forms of experience and successfully did so.[21] Much modern art may see its role as to promote, at all levels, the development and aspiration of the instincts, all round a firm grasp of a total world of experience, resulting in a proud confidence. This means a cultural reform legitimating exotic values. The effect would be similar to the Neo-Platonic philosophy at the Renaissance, an opening up of new possible values, new possible ways of living.

Those who wish to concern themselves solely with the understanding may well speak of magic as a 'forbidden science'. A doctrine of will is not an aid to the understanding, nor is it intended as such. A magical cosmology is not so much a metaphysic as means of acquiring power. Yet magic does not reject orthodoxy, it uses it as a point of permanent reference and stability. So it employs concepts which are arbitrary, long passages of gibberish (anathema to the understanding) barbarous names of evocation and suchlike. Yet magic is far from anti-thetical to understanding; unlike the witch, the mage does not sell his soul to attain power. Magical books are to be kept hidden from the unworthy. The magician gives a personal interpretation to Gnostic myth.

The magician cultivates an internal aesthetic, not caring what others think of it. There is an almost deliberate embrace of something that may look like failure. Magic explores strange whims of the will, like opium fancies, possibilities barely ventured in our culture. All original art is akin to madness, on paths untrodden one is on one's own, the multitude will decry. As one moves into the unaccounted, one is doing that the validity of which conventional wisdom or sanity has always denied. Sanity is judged by the experience of the multitude, and their experience can never encapsulate untried possibility even by formulae however liberal.

What we may call high magic has noble, if still selfish aspirations. High Magic involves the aspiration for all experience, or at least a representative sample of the most basic forms, to bring them under the power of the individual, make them all accessible, learning how to utilise the whole range of possible human reactions to situations. Typically the artist takes up one stand, identifies himself by his relentless opposition to some opposite point of view. Instead he might try to contain all points of view within his outlook, even when he is only concerned to express a segment of what he understands as whole truth. The part will gain from the instinctual truth of the whole. With the integration of philosophy and magic we develop a science of learning all possible reactions.

We might compare rising through the spheres and rising through the outlooks, the determining factors. One aspires to a higher form of certainty and satisfaction, a complete liberation in the psychological sense. Particular paths limit energy, the aim of high magic is to reach a condition where the will is not so limited, where it may take its fill of a comprehensive cross section of the forms human beliefs and values may take.

The law of Thelema is for the few and secret. Magick offers the form of a personal religion. The only justification for accepting orthodox religion is laziness and conformity. Magick can provide the ritual and formulae one loses by rejecting a common church. The magician is the true religious individualist, the ultra Protestant perhaps.

To say the universe is filled with diabolical plots and traps is to evoke what is said in the Goetia about the perils of allowing the various demons any more leeway than that permitted to them by the ritual. King Solomon bound the seventy-two evil spirits of the Goetia into a brass vessel solely because of their pride. Those of Babylon broke open the vessel and the spirits escaped. Solomon was a monotheist, ruler of a monotheistic empire, Babylon was curiosity and magic, open rather than closed, polytheistic. Solomon shut up the spirits perhaps to do honour to his own God because the spirits claimed to be self-subsistent, and would be wreckers of the System. Babylonian magicians replaced external protection against the spirits by a personal and individual protection. Theirs was not a prohibition on experience but rather encouragement to have it while guarding yourself against possible evil effects. Solomon shut them up not because of fear but for aesthetic purposes.

If we use Frazerian accounts of magic in our analysis of the attraction of certain ideas we must refuse to base our own case on any such attraction. Ideas that appeal to you are likely to have no appeal to others. Any number of exciting ideas you write down leave others cold. Magic can work through power of sympathy, understanding the secret of playing on the suggestibility of a subject, working him up to an emotional pitch. It is a demonstrable fact that magic can work, especially when we think of the great range of mental experiences that might become open to us. History is a vast treasure house of possible human experience. What we call magic is a means of tapping this treasure.

Rationalistic magic is not incompatible with scepticism and analytical philosophy. The magical approach of Neo-Platonism, because it is designed to answer to human desires does not exclude rationalism, even of the austerest kind. It is a function of rational magic to offer emotional satisfactions for all points of view. There is a magical technique for satisfying pride, for visiting Hell, like Aeneas, Dante, Virgil, and Odysseus, while remaining unscathed. We see the point of the pure and simplistic morality of the magician.

Crowley's view of the world is magical. He does not disbelieve in immortality nor any other idea that may appeal to the minds of men. He holds out a hope of existence as pure joy through the magical freedom of all possible ideas. There is a materialistic inertia that impedes this. It is felt that our values are determined by extraneous factors, and it is these factors that need to be changed if we wish to see a change in our values. The way to overcome repressive values is through the magical philosophy, not through such magical hopes, (utopian schemes etc). The magical philosopher could come to fill the role of a priest, but a singularly non repressive kind of priest.

High magic, rational magic is trying to effect change by the dissemination of ideas. If it is desired to see in existence some particular value then the magician endeavours to promote it directly, rather than hoping that some predicted change in material circumstances will have that effect. This was what the Neo-Platonists did at the Renaissance. In many respects society at the end of the middle ages felt old and tired. New values, it was felt, could be created.

Renaissance Neo-Platonism offered an allegorical esoteric interpretation of dogma together with a magical idea of manipulating ideas and concepts to produce desired specific effects. Western esotericism still offers an image of understanding, with resistance to the tyranny of fashion. All values are generated from a rational principle with magic and mysticism at the heart of it. The appeal of the magic infuses society as a whole with philosophical meaning of which the primary function is to draw away from immediate prejudice. It should not be treated as superstition. It is the preservation of a wisdom in the face of all the forces ranged against it. Magic is exciting because it appeals so strongly to the desires.

Conscious Magick affects the attitude to the ideas current in society, bringing the sense that these are manipulable, that to a great extent our desires for culture and society may be met by a suitable manipulation of intellectual ideas, that the ideas and values we entertain may to a greater extent than is often realised be open to alteration in the service of the will.

It is customary to assert that magic is mistaken science, but it is more than that. Pure science is disinterested enquiry, applied science or technology is the provision of means to ends, magic is concerned with the satisfaction of desire. Magical technique is the means taken to procure satisfaction of desire. We see how magic can come to provide a polar alternative to religion. In general it can be said that religion is a system for the regulation, direction and control of desire, therefore it is the case that the outlook underlying magical practice is unamenable to religious constraint.

There are many kinds of magic. Magic lacks the objectivity of science, its aims are different. Scientific knowledge is formalisable, magical knowledge is subjective, closely related to desire. By the standards of religion, magic is actively immoral. But magical knowledge is also useful knowledge. It is useful to know speedy ways to the accomplishment of one's desires. By its nature magical knowledge cannot be common.

Magical technique is an important and universal feature of human society, as should be more clearly recognised. Throughout history the magician has been a recognised type. Many of his accomplishments were perfectly real, however dependent on the conventions of his society. In itself magical technique may be morally neutral, but its general use may be the mark of an outlook directly anti-thetical to the religious.

Maya Deren wrote in *The Voodoo Gods* :-

"the best condition for magical action is not the primitive community with its collective emphasis, but the modern community with its individualistic emphasis, and it is here that one may experience the pre-eminent spectacle of the magician at work. He conceives his plans in almost solitary secrecy, or with a few cohorts; he is feverishly protective of the exclusive right to exploit the power of his discovery or invention; he is frequently concerned with an almost occult effort to divine that special twist of public taste which makes for a hit or a best-seller; he is devoted to the idea of a magic combination of words in a certain just so order, which is a catchy slogan. He labours to create a skilfully obsessive image of material or sexual seduction, and is not above accomplishing this with a maximum of artifice and connotative sleight of hand; he is involved in a complex and formal series of cabbala like manipulations involving 'contacts' publicity incantations and even what might accurately be termed the cocktail libation." [22]

I think she is a bit unkind to the perennial archetype of the magician. The magician is after power, but power of a special kind. He has a fascination with secrecy for its own sake. In modern society he will like to have an involvement with the secret service, to be some kind of secret agent. He is preoccupied with numerology, with esoteric and mystic codes. He is obsessed with charisma, sexual seduction and hypnosis, with making his own will prevail. Crowley exemplifies this archetype in modern society. In history there were Dee, Cagliostro, even Casanova. The magician's character is a complex of features that tend to go together, though sometimes there are bits left out. Some magicians want to be notable for their chastity, as did Paracelsus.

Magically speaking, evil is not a choice one takes. For good may control evil, but if evil controls good it destroys it. Evil is destructive hatred. It has its place in the fulfilment of the subject, but not to the end of his own destruction. When evil and its antithesis (good) are together made to subserve a higher goal, that must be conceived as itself good, for it cannot be evil. It is a magical objective to permit the manifestation of each of the forces of evil and compel them to serve the will of the magician, understood as good.

There are things one gives up for the sake of the Great Work. Some might appear like moral renunciations. The magician, for example forswears injustice and untruthfulness. There are good reasons why the magician is not possessed by the unworthy motives that govern lesser mortals. A moral weakness is the sacrifice of a long term for a short term gain. It is the will divided against itself. Part of the essence of his vocation is that such short term gains simply do not appeal to him, they are not desired, they would not satisfy.

He renounces injustice because he no longer feels inclined to commit it. All his activity serves his major will. Satisfaction outside that major current is not possible to him. The apparent exception to this rule is when his will, i.e. his major current, is concerned with overthrow or amendment of current moral conceptions. Then ordinary moral virtues may come to appear limiting and restricting and needing to be transcended. Strictly speaking this is a different question. What is involved are matters of symbolism and terminology. While generally the magician will probably prefer to be described as just, in specialised cases he may perceive that character as a limitation. This is not to say his is unjust in the original sense. What is at issue is the description which we are to apply to him.

The black magician has advanced some degree on the road to enlightenment, but has reached the point where, confronted with the freedom of the void, he is overwhelmed by it. He feels a need to justify himself for being what he is, but he cannot find anything on which to pin any such justification. Nor can he think of anything he could become, in which his being would be justified. Without a shred of justification on which to pin his being, he would normally become incapable of action, sinking further and further into the Abyss, into ever deepening circles of dilemma, disintegration and despair. By turning his face away from the need for justification, which he inwardly knows to be overwhelming, he creates for himself, in the Abyss, a mockery of a self-sufficient being. That which he cannot be he will use his powers to play at being. He has a particular hatred for all creatures who advance to a stage of enlightenment beyond that which he himself has reached. The only form of life he can satisfactorily live is one which involves maiming restricting and destroying other more genuine forms. He has no positive charge. In a futile attempt to overcome his emptiness he desperately tries to destroy everything that is not himself. Above all he fights reason. He can only will by destroying. It is not that he derives a philosophical pleasure from destroying, like De Sade's heroes, only that if he does not destroy he will perish and worse.

Crowleyan Magick has a solitary, introverted quality when one works on one's own writings. There is something almost subjective in the concentration on my own thought, my own experience, my own life. There is much about Magick that other people regard as schizoid. One forges ones own weapon, invents one's own religion, one's own scriptures. Magick is the primaeval alternative to religion, to God. There is a problem with shattering tradition, one cannot just get rid of Christianity. The primal truth of the magical world view is like an extreme individualism.

For Crowley, Wagner's Parsifal was a work of great Magickal significance. Religion relates to the sense of highest aesthetic unity. Wagner's power to manipulate these raptures are of the greatest significance for thought and culture. Understanding how to manipulate such emotion, prescribing its precise nature and quality is better by far than yielding to it. Wagner can give the impression of great depth and great wisdom. He was a sort of Klingsor with balls. The ultimate object, the holy grail or philosopher's stone, is the extraction of maximum enjoyment from life as lived. He employs psychological categories such as are found in Freud. His descendant Gottfried Wagner[23] says that he is central to the German soul, with its need for redemption. What this might suggest is that the German soul is something created, ruled by magic. As well as a seducer, Wagner was a magician, Nietzsche said, and Crowley would have approved.[24]

Crowley writes of a grave crisis concerning the schools of magic.[17] There is a crisis in the conflict between the black and the white schools. The white school of magic comes from Europe, he says. In seeking a positive philosophy of life, white magic, one does think in terms of some form of creativity, or historical action. Western Christianity actually provided this on the historical stage with a man like Cromwell. But as well as the white and the black there is the idea of yellow magic, a brilliant clarification. The *Tao te Ching*, for example is not mystical or political but a magical treatise. It is so gratifying because it promises everything through the unexpected and paradoxical path of non action.

# Philosophy proper

"His time has been spent in three very distinct manners: the Secret Way of the Initiate, the Path of Poetry and

Philosophy, and the Open Sea of Romance and Adventure."[25]

The archetype of the philosopher is of someone who is a constant and continual prey to doubts, which he repels by argument. In this sense he is not like the sage or guru (Initiate), he is not serene. The philosopher is a being cold and abstracted, often he is inhuman. He is like the mathematician in that he deals with abstractions. The philosopher is not to be thought of as subordinated to the truth in the way that any authentic artist must be. He is the juggler in the Tarot pack, he makes the intangible manipulable. The philosopher, it is said, must communicate his wisdom, write it down. This is presumably that he may clearly be seen to be a philosopher. Otherwise no one will believe that he is, and his persistent unreasonableness will be seen as self-delusion, or will even be such. Amateurs in philosophy are perceived as the most utter wasters one could imagine, upholders of exploded arguments.

People who attack philosophy generally do so because they wish to enshrine some philosophically dubious assumption under the aegis of authority. In certain professions, one is effectively expected to swallow various questionable philosophical ideas as part of the training. Philosophical ideas certainly have a most influential part to play in society, and are often used in an authoritarian way. The principle of dogmatic authority is widely used, even in a society which professes to reject it. To suppress ideas without refuting them is simply to load them with the pain of frustrated desire.

A philosophy gives a set of values and attitudes. Many of the judgments delivered by people like architects, lawyers, journalists, politicians, art critics, presume a form of spiritual authority that can be seen as depending in upon contentious philosophical assumptions. Through philosophy one will be able to expose much of the hocus pocus of professionals. Philosophy undermines the esoteric secrets of the separate professions.

Philosophy is necessary to uproot presuppositions. Philosophical ideas are intimately involved in the progress of civilisation. Where there is not good philosophy there is bad philosophy and dogmatism. These are an oppression on the mind and an obstruction to healthy ambition. Faults in society and culture, aesthetic flaws as in architecture, and political flaws, as with the understanding of liberty, all come down to basic philosophical questions. Only these can generate adequate authoritative judgements. Otherwise there are only opinions to balance against other opinions. One may put religion in place of philosophy but that is even more controversial.

Crude worldly ambition pursues success according to the current scale of values. It resents philosophy as the attempt to put into question that scale. Such questions throw into doubt the whole value of achievement, threaten the self-image of the successful. The criticism is made that philosophy springs from envy and resentment as if that is an unnecessary motive that we can well do without. The ruling classes traditionally are uninterested in ideas. It is ideas that threaten to rob them of their privilege. Yet any proposal for a reordering of experience must be interesting, as it would bring about a prospect of rational conscious control, as against passive acceptance. Socrates managed to persuade many of the Athenian aristocrats that philosophy was more exciting than debauchery. He was disturbing, offensive and destructive. Intellectual and philosophical systems are ways of producing equivalents of aristocratic pride.

The philosophical impulses spring from the personality, including the sort of psychological drives on which Freud had much to say. When the intelligent young student looks at what appear to be power structures currently in place he may see irritating irrationality and tyranny, questionable assumptions upon which everything appears to proceed. He is sure that he could do better, he aspires to a kind of power, making his ideas have effect in society. He imagines a society of like-minded friends with him who have come to essentially the same conclusions.

Nietzsche proposed the idea of a transvaluation of all values. Philosophers of the future will bring all values under surveillance. One aspires to philosophy as the supreme organising rational principle. The programme would be for a culture which flows down from such a principle. The enlightened elite would maintain a constant sense of responsibility to the people, instructing them in the manifold forms of freedom, but above all they would uphold the position of their philosophy within society.

The communication of philosophy to the people is a job arguably as necessary as that of the philosopher himself. Perhaps this means rather the communication of the role of the philosopher, transmitting a respect for the role of the philosopher to gain for him an appropriate sphere of power. Crowley honoured popularisers like T H Huxley, and even Herbert Spencer.

The Secret Chiefs are one mythical expression of such an ideal, as were the Rosicrucians and the Illuminati.[26] Rationalists turn themselves into a ruling class, propound the principles of their philosophy and fight for them, so that they may survive and flourish. A rationalistic ideal might involve a small body of people in all walks of life committed to philosophy and its propagation. We might envisage a class of illuminated ones dedicated to a rational idea, fully conscious of all methods of conditioning and persuasion, individual and mass and fully resistant to demoralisation, accepting that there is no idea that we could not somehow come to believe. Such an ideal, of course, will be far from immune to criticism.

Crowley's plans for the general reformation of civilisation, have obvious philosophical implications. Also his philosophy has a role to play as psychopomp, as a guide for the individual soul. Civilisation at its best has had a deep respect for philosophy, Plato, Aristotle, Confucius, Lao Tsu, the Upanishads, the Buddhist canon, where fundamental questions are discussed profoundly. Some take the ancient Chandogya Upanishad as model of philosophising. Sometimes what the philosopher is looking for is a special kind of certainty. His argumentation leads us away progressively from the things of this world where it is not to be found to the mystical realms where it is.

Crowley is not only interested in the sort of philosophy that would seem to support mysticism and magic. He is not primarily teaching building blocks for a metaphysical system of his own. Much philosophy is concerned with ugly hateful ideas that have to be repelled. Insofar as anti-metaphysical philosophy seeks to establish the right and solidity of ideas and purposes independently of metaphysical justification, it supports freedom and the right to deviate. It is also an aggressive weapon of great power.

Ideas like the Kabbalah and Neo-Platonism are attacked by philosophers. Historians of philosophy tell us that Descartes or some other philosopher rendered such ideas outmoded. Berkeley and Hume we are told have been long refuted. Philosophy aspires to grab hold of your real innermost beliefs, throw all into doubt and remake you.

Academic analytical philosophy involves a serious attack on the fashionable alternatives to received opinion that can be as irritating as received opinion to the rebelliously minded. Philosophy offers the individual access to a perspective outside the prevailing ideas and values of his own milieu, and a point from which these may be effectively resisted. Contemporary philosophy as taught in British and American universities supposedly offers pure intellectual thought, unobstructed by arbitrary power structures.

However, quasi religious claims are made for such philosophy to the effect that all ambition should be satisfied therein. There is even the suggestion of a kind of official wisdom, advocating reconciliation to the status quo. One may find that what in fact orthodox philosophy does say about values is distinctly unsympathetic. Bourgeois values, as distinct from mere abstract intellectual questions, may repel. We can see the emotional appeal of revolution as an understandable expression of resentment, and as linking up intellectual and emotional needs effectively.

Yet one may commend analytical philosophy as intellectual discipline, even when likely to be rejected by it. Whatever its faults, modern academic philosophy sets high standards of argument. Such standards can be very easy to lose. Then we end up with the arbitrariness of so much continental philosophy with many competing claims to wisdom.

One thing young people look to philosophy for is wisdom, guidance in how to live life. Some say this is not the role of philosophy but of religion. Artists may offer such wisdom. Traditional philosophy derives conclusions about the purpose of life from reflections about the nature of the world. This is a reason why Heidegger is so attractive. Existentialism offers poetic vision, a type of emotion, suggesting the oriental tradition of sages. Actually Heidegger's concept of authenticity is not dissimilar to the Thelemic concept of the true will.

The Thelemite will need to reconcile his will and aspiration with the most up to date philosophy. Crowley's interest in the history of philosophy, in its power to challenge received thought, would not stop at any position philosophy had reached in his own lifetime. As we have seen he was interested in Russell, who moved philosophy on beyond Absolute Idealism, and beyond Russell there was Wittgenstein and his followers like Gilbert Ryle,[27] who dominated philosophy in England in the years after his death.

Ordinary people do not live under false philosophy, they live under no philosophy. It is not the job of philosophy to criticise experience nor yet to restrict it in any possible way. What Crowley initially asks of philosophy is that it should open us to all possibilities of thought, feeling and experience, breaking down limits rather than setting us tasks. He wants to make more easily possible the joy of yielding to the fascination of innumerable different ideas without getting ensnared by them. He is particularly concerned with bringing what he calls the wisdom of the East to the West. This does not mean adopting a philosophy of eclecticism, or pick and mix. If you simply pick out attractive bits from the history of philosophy you will be open to immediate challenge from those who argue that what you have chosen has been superseded, thoroughly refuted. Immediately you will be forced into serious defensive argument.

Like genes, the philosophy of Thelema may be dominant or recessive. It is recessive when allowing other possibilities, even shallow ones, to work. In its political form it becomes dominant. In this place it is intolerant, merciless in the protection of its recessive sister.

All this, however, is to emphasise the benevolent aspect of the philosophical will, not the raw ambition which comes out when any obstacle is encountered. The lust for power of the thinker is as marked as that of the politician who hypocritically intones that all he asks is 'the right to serve'. Though I present my idea as if with the best will in the world, as if all I want to do is to contribute to the good of mankind, there is always an element of disingenuousness. If truth had no part to play Crowleyanity could hardly cope with a strong motive against it. Unconstrained by truth a philosophical theory is like a thesis in the air. Truth is more constraining than the very best of arbitrary hypotheses. Its primary quality is its negativity, convicting an opposing view of actual falsehood or its equivalent.

The suggestion is put that angry, negative and destructive behaviour is the product of inevitable frustration at unrealistic hopes and ambitions. This further contributes to Crowley's reputation as a bad person. If someone could show him he were wrong, that would not be unbearable, nor even especially painful, it might perhaps come as a kind of relief. But if someone tells him he shall come to see himself as wrong only after some acutely painful crisis involving repression and denial of what he most strongly thinks and feels then he resists that as much as he can. In his resistance he may appear a Hitlerian figure,[28] aiming to overcome others with the force of his will. Every alternative seems to him deeply unsatisfactory. Yet his formula, what a strange and useless thing it is? Could it be the completest folly?[29] How could he envisage it taking effect in the life of the individual or of society? In a religious sense it makes pathways for desire.

It seems that there is tremendous pressure on the individual not to resist what seems wrong to him. An idea makes demands for the belief of those who find it attractive and those who do not. Why should I accept any idea which I find unattractive, or expect anyone else to accept ideas which I find attractive but which they may not? In many cases the reasons are clear cut. What we may call reality or the material world may obtrude. But in some cases there are a great many alternatives on offer. What has to be made clear is the extreme offensiveness of inadequately grounded authority.

Magical thought introduces mythology into philosophy, much as the Kabbalah does into Judaism. The most intractable dilemmas and paradoxes of ambitious thought find expression in myths about Oedipus, the Crucifixion, the Great Boyg,[30] the Dweller on the Threshold, or Choronzon. From some points of view philosophy is engaged in an impossible, even diabolic task. There is curiosity and its paralysis, then the various solutions. Sometimes a solution can work for others but not for the philosopher who devised it. Crowley's Magickal system with all its grades of initiation, its temple building and weapon making, all can be seen as a mythologising of philosophy.

The tremendous originality of Greek philosophy lay not in the finding of bad reasons for what we believe by instinct (Bradley) but in capturing in a form acceptable to the rational intellect some of the important insights of religious intuition. The thread goes from Orpheus to the Pythagoreans to Plato, eventually back into myth with a figure like Apollonius of Tyana. If philosophy is conceived as a quest for ultimate truth pursued by purely deductive steps it may come to seem a futile quest, symbolised by Magritte's *La Lampe Philosophique*, in which the philosopher appears to be smoking his own nose. Rational criticism is a means of reconciling conflicting outlooks. An outlook that cannot defend itself rationally must fall, for reason is the ground of all dialogue, but in a form that presupposes instinct and intuition, making their discoveries explicitly intelligible. A metaphysical discovery is not arrived at by deductive logic but elucidated by it.

Some philosophers, like the Pythagoreans, seem to derive much of their inspiration from the flash of mystical illumination. Where this is so the philosophy is often an attempt to explain the illumination, and should not be interpreted as if it were merely built up from observations made on the terrestrial level, as if even the concept of enlightenment is something that was devised by analogy with the mundane.

Mysticism may be taken as involving the principle that such doctrines are only to be understood from the vantage point of certain abnormal states of consciousness. Against this it may be said that the idea of the One can be grasped and conceived philosophically. The basic concepts around which mysticism works are constructed or revealed by the intellect. However the complete removal of perplexity will be an intense subjective experience. Such perfect understanding after its intellectual delineation remains in a sense an object of aspiration, a kind of image of fulfilment and ecstasy. So philosophy comes to involve itself with the postulation of a psychological condition 'complete understanding', the One, the insight drained of all possible predicates (though still perhaps too much).

The One of Plotinus may be a worthy object for philosophy. The One may be characterised as the resolution of perplexity. We might apply it to Gilbert Ryle's programme for the resolution of perplexity in the philosophy of mind. The One could be characterised as that philosophical insight or the object of that philosophical insight that resolves philosophical perplexity concerning the nature and origin of that which is. Yet insofar as the One is postulated as existing it generates its opposite. There are sudden panics, fear of insanity, of a solipsistic universe, as understanding proceeds and insight becomes clearer.

> "It may end in real insanity, which concludes the activities of the Adept during this present life, or by his rebirth into his own body and mind with the simplicity of a little child."[31]

In their very different ways Gilbert Ryle, Nagarjuna and the Neo-Platonists, all come to the same conclusion.[32] The 'One' the insight, is in a sense void, it is nothing. It is a state of understanding, but that is all that could be said about it. Understanding, philosophical understanding, *is* just understanding. It has no particular content. Certainly it is the antithesis of perplexity, and it gains its strength from this, for we are most of the time at least moderately perplexed and it is the overcoming of this resistance. Such understanding has long been conceived as desirable as indeed it is. But then what more is there for philosophy to do? Other states of mind can be conceived which are also desirable. Can we be helped onto the attainment of conditions of intense happiness? Philosophy becomes magic, philosophy linked to desire.

The question of how your soul is to find peace is not strictly a philosophical question. What philosophy can do is to act as a tool of power, and therefore the enjoyment of power, which can be that extra final ingredient which brings happiness.

From a magical viewpoint, even the harm supposed to have been done by philosophers, can provide a motive for admiring them. Aristotle, Bacon, Rousseau or Descartes, have all been charged with responsibility for catastrophic forms of dissociation. Arguably errors of such magnitude are even more valuable than truths. They suggest the creativity of Maya, the illusion that the Hindus thought produces the world.

Efforts to think beyond the limitations of ordinary language are illegitimate logical and grammatical error, according to many modern philosophers. Such views tend to discount the historical importance of philosophy, as for eighteenth century Britain when the culture was philosophy driven. Utilitarian philosophy, together with the Enlightenment doctrine of psychological egoism, can be seen as having provided the foundation for British industrial civilisation. Philosophy can provide a programme for civilisation and culture. In Ancient Rome there were stoics versus epicureans, and in England there were intuitionists versus utilitarians. Increasing democratisation means that philosophical ideas cease to have directing force. Popular conceptions and misconceptions acquire the same weight as clear philosophical ideas. Modern ideas are plebeian ideas, ideas which only scratch the surface of things, but to which the mass are attracted.

Arguably the truest manifestation of European civilisation consists in its philosophical systems, which provide the basic programmes for life and development. Understand these and we understand much of why civilisation is as it is, now as in the Middle Ages when Aristotle's doctrine of substance provided the foundation of thought.

If much of Descartes seems obvious and natural is this just because his philosophy has penetrated so thoroughly into our culture and education? Descartes' is itself a scholastic type philosophy, concerned with science and possible knowledge. There are those who believe that Descartes can be unravelled and some of the deep problems of our culture can thereby be solved. According to Frances Yates, Descartes was guilty of a most superficial dismissal of the problems of mind because he wanted to establish mechanism as the principle of science.[33] Often philosophers uninterested in some particular field make a few dogmatic remarks about it, giving rise to subsequent great confusion among their followers.

The really ambitious philosopher does not simply aspire to produce a set of intellectual concepts ingeniously strung together, the opium inspired aim of Coleridge and others of the second division.[34] He wants to be able to guide people by inspiration to a mode of life that feels perfectly satisfactory. Insofar as philosophers ever manage to achieve this, it is through their ability to convey the feeling that truth has been found. This is the ultimate oracle, the philosopher's stone, philosophy's claim to ultimate truth. Magic can have a part to play here in producing the illusion that this has been achieved.

To find Aristotelianism satisfactory philosophy, or any system complete and satisfactory, is like abandoning the philosophic impulse. Orthodoxy here is perhaps even more classic than what we find in Hegel. There is nothing to be said to someone who does not feel oppressed by the completeness of this system.[35] To him Dante is perfect and Milton is perverse. To others, though an adequate philosophy will repress and contain this dissident impulse.

There are philosophers who simply offer us a set of concepts which they think fruitful. Yet anyone who says there is nothing but persuasion and includes himself in that confesses himself to hold beliefs on inadequate grounds, and to be content to do so. That is unphilosophical and slavish. Where rhetoric ends philosophy begins. True philosophy can only arise from combative aggression. The philosopher is more ambitious than the politician. Part of the object is to get accepted, find admirers, establish a niche for himself, get away with what he wants to say. The philosopher must not be like the politician, content with a limited following and prepared to disregard those who oppose him radically. Argument should convince even those who do not want to be convinced.

Philosophy has been brought to an end over and over again by whoever does not rise up to it and rests happy with a dogma that is not subjected to argument. There is a need for genuine philosophy to break the hold of compulsive metaphysical arguments, however interesting. Only intense aggression makes for discontent with dogma and refusal to submit to its jurisdiction. With this motive one sees power, a reality that others deny. It would seem that philosophy will come to and end when there are no more geniuses. Then established views will no longer be challenged. Already we detect mediocrity even of most philosophers. To rest content with any gulf of disagreement, to leave philosophical theory at the level of hypothesis is a failure of the aggressive impulse. Contentment with something just left in the air, to take a position when an opposite position holds an equal claim is a betrayal of philosophy.

Of all the philosophers who opened up interesting worlds, Kant was of particular interest to Crowley, because of his magical implications and the creative possibilities of his thought. Metaphysics is concerned with what ultimately is. Kant writes of unknowable things in themselves, yet suggests that in a sense we may create realities by the exercise of the moral will. Kant's whole philosophy may be seen as a way of making room for freewill. The claim to freewill involves a quite astonishing metaphysical arrogance, as if the laws of cause and effect are themselves a constraint and one wants a magical power to control everything. Freud's speculations about infantile fantasies of omnipotence may have some bearing on the subject. To say this is not to attack mysticism in favour of mundane reality, far from it. It is gratifying and pleasurable in so many ways, but the extent to which Kant takes morality removes it quite from the 'invisible hand'. It suggests that morality is something that has to be directly willed.

Genghis Khan had his own ideas as to the greatest joy in life.[37] An alternative view is that it is pre-eminently the philosopher who is able to understand a life ideal in its satisfying potential. The destructive power of scepticism, meaning not only Hume, but also the paralysing confusion induced by prolonged exposure to much different philosophical argument, is a weapon in the service of lofty ambition. Philosophy offers the hope of some distinctive pleasures. There is the hope of exercising a kind of leadership, to prescribe in advance what is to be said and done, to emancipate oneself from depressing thoughts, to increase the freedom and possibilities of one's own mind, as those of the minds of others. There is an urge to say something earth shattering and profound. There is sexual excitement in the philosopher's will to persuade. He is unable to accept a place and position required of him. Thus there is an issue about specifically the philosopher's sexuality. His work is different from that of other creative people.

The philosopher's concepts closely match his desires and inclinations. With an urgent present desire it seems that it must be satisfied before any kind of contentment is possible. To have a philosophy can come to seem an urgent necessity. To undermine a philosophical solution is not to create discontent and confusion, at least not necessarily. Contentment is not only the result of satisfactory philosophical theories. There are other ways to get it.

When self-assertion itself is channelled, after initially successful rebellion, into socially conformist channels, it is then that the great spirit must choose solitude, distancing himself from the mass. On his criticism depends his whole security. He feels he has to have theories, beliefs, to justify himself, confusing self-assertion with beliefs and theories. Any bliss is assumed to be the reward of his thought. Yet even his thought is only another possibility, one could have an alternative thought. Why therefore is this thought true? It is his paranoid defensiveness that leads him to try and justify every single thing, every thing that he is.

He feels he is in a condition that depends on his ideas about it, Without his ideas he feels, he is in danger of going under.

> "Since all things soever are separate; since their separateness is the essential element of their existence; and since all are equally illusions, why aspire to the Holy Guardian Angel? — why not to the Dweller on the Threshold? To the man who has not passed entirely through the Abyss thoughts of this kind are positively frightful. There is no rational answer possible, from the nature of the case; and I was tormented indescribably by these thoughts, thousands after thousands, each a terrific thunderbolt blasting its way through my brain during these frightful months."[38]

He feels that as the very pre-condition of his being he must have a theory. He closes himself off from simple direct experience because he needs defences against being swamped or drowned.

The philosopher is in search of something, as are the art student and the mystic. Searching for Mysteries, trying to uncover Mysteries, one easily goes the wrong way about it. Simpler people may get to Mystery towards which you struggle earnestly and fruitlessly.

Philosophy continues, even after Wittgenstein is supposed to have dissolved it. For one thing it remains as a career structure. Diversity of opinion was something which philosophers of the past aspired to bring to an end. Searing discontent continues as the motive for philosophy, frustration and resentment. We start off with the premise of a massive disharmony and a vague hope of aesthetic consolation.

Learning philosophy, you attach yourself to some power structure and train yourself in the defensive arguments. Looking at it this way, originality may appear free spiritedness while humbler work, expository work, may seem a form of thraldom. There is submissiveness, humility and submission to other people's values even in the realm of philosophy where there are more choices perhaps than in some other disciplines. In whatever work you are expected to do, how much of your true feelings are to be expressed and how much repressed? People justify themselves by a claim to virtue. The will to communicate is closely allied to the will to dominate.

Philosophers are to be seen as guardians of the conditions on which discussion is carried on, not even so much as umpires as points of reference. Theirs is an understanding of the conditions of wisdom, of many kinds of highest aspiration. Even if it makes no difference to the truth of anything that has been said before, practical consequences flow from its acceptance. Philosophy has value in promoting spiritual states, including scepticism and mental paralysis. Philosophy is also an attack on religion, and on one's own beliefs insofar as they seem to depend upon questionable philosophical arguments. But anything can return as language game.

Because of the impossibility of knowing anything more than a small segment of philosophy there is inevitably much ignorance, even on matters one wants to talk about. In the great movement of nineteenth century German metaphysics minor figures like Stirner and Von Hartmann are actually very significant. Academic philosophers take the matter differently and treat them as negligible. Mainstream philosophy ignores such minor figures, quite often because it comes to embody vast assumptions and presupposes the rightness of one side in the argument. To look at just the major figures as if they represented the whole philosophy of the time is to miss out crucial minor figures who were essential to the whole discussion that was being carried on. Yet as Crowley writes in *Liber Aleph* in relation to the classics.

> "And these Books have lived long and become famous because they are the Fruits of ancient Trees whereof thou art directly the Heir, wherefrom (say I) they are more truly germane to thine own Nature than Books of Collateral Offshoots, though such were in themselves better and wiser."[39]

There are only a few philosophies that have real grandeur and greatness. Nietzsche's does, Schopenhauer's does, Hegel's does, to speak of the moderns. If the ultimate ambition of a philosopher is to be the originator of a great system, Aquinas, Lull, Kant, Hegel would all imagine themselves to have done that. Wittgenstein imposed his presumptions upon a culture. All great systems have their virtues, but in dialogue with one another.

A great thinker has a power in him that greatly transcends his capacity to be understood, he is influential for something other than what he really means to say. Thus arises the peculiar feature that someone can maintain that a great philosopher has been completely misunderstood and that he really meant the opposite of what everybody always took him to have been saying. So if he didn't really say what everybody admired him for, shouldn't that mean he is irrelevant, that he didn't really speak for his time at all? In fact he is of more interest than ever.

Although Wittgensteinian philosophy from one viewpoint is an assault on sceptical doubt, from another it is quite the opposite. There is denial of all that is not 'ordinary language', an attack on all pretension, all aspirations, all exceptional experience. Extreme philosophical scepticism is directed against any comforting faith. The implication is that it all may rest upon an illegitimate assumption, and unjustified extrapolation. Pursued to a logical extreme this is disturbing, even terrifying. Philosophy is a ruthless criticism of experience. 'Ordinary' experience it may well leave in place, it may see it as its purpose to leave it in place. Extraordinary experience, however, is another question. Philosophy may appear as some brutal instrument.

Such philosophy can suggest ugly chaos instead of present beliefs, a Sartrean contingency, a very disturbing atheistic thought. Imagine undermining all the assumptions that make for the comfort of religion to the extent that even your sexual pleasure is alleged to rest upon unjustified assumptions. Any healthy, straightforward delight, philosophy undermines with doubt. Yet certainty is not a psychological impossibility. Paralysing doubt rests upon an assumption.

> "And yet doubt is a good servant but a bad master, a perfect mistress but a nagging wife."[39]

That a question has to be answered, that an opposing idea has to be considered, is itself a form of assumption, like the idea that every act of will has to be justified by truth. Once on this track there is no escape.

> "Enough of because! Be he damned for a dog."[40]

That there is another way of being is known from experience, one that resists or ignores the moralistic assaults, shelves all such questions, refrains from approaching them. Yet the assaults of philosophy upon experience are valuable lessons. In them there is great power. One should derive one's right not to consider every opposing idea from an original aggression, not from a search for 'truth' outside the self. Philosophy makes you consider every opposing idea to those in which you take comfort.

Philosophy can have a number of different roles to play. There is the resolution of intellectual perplexity. There is the Baconian ideal, a programme for applied science and technology. Then there is a further possible role, the seminal role, that of supplying the concepts which are to underlie all the various aspects of a culture. This is not to include Collingwood's conception, that of describing absolute presuppositions. Philosophy begets sciences but some perhaps are misbegotten. Pseudo science firmly enough established, has a life of its own.

Colin Wilson, who was somewhat taken with Crowley, proposed a conception of philosophy as 'raising consciousness'. We may think of intellectual activity as helping to secure pleasure and satisfaction by helping to overcome some of the great mass of tension that oppresses the mind. Such tensions are brought about by the oppressive half truths that do not fit either our desires or our perceptions but in which we are pressured to acquiesce for the sake of others. For some classes of people spiritual freedom is of no concern. They do not feel the oppression because they value something else more highly, the removal of doubt and the power of action.

One motive for philosophy is to be recognised as a genius. In British philosophy a genius is successful revolutionary. Academic philosophy in Britain is about as anti-democratic an institution as it is possible to get. That is part of its appeal. The rewards of the genius are so much the greater. G E Moore and Russell overthrew Bradley. Then came Wittgenstein. The path of the rebel is most difficult of all, but the reward of success is like absolute power. British analytical philosophers are a strange set of people, curiously limited in some respects, drenched in a particular tradition, of which Russell's papers on Bradley were one crucial part, almost in some ways suffering under it. There is tremendous conformist pressure, and while a great many impulses can be satisfied there are a great many more that cannot.

G E Moore has been compared to Prince Myshkin,[41] stressing his lack of the perversity of mind that inspired previous revolutionaries like Bradley or Mctaggart. He was very important for philosophy and English culture generally. We can appreciate this even while loathing the preciousness of Bloomsbury and its heirs. We may just value the purely intellectual destruction of Hegelianism.

We may distinguish the determining or legislative function of philosophy from the understanding one. When thought is free it really can underpin experience, which is what Plato really means, it can create experience itself. However, to stick to the determining aspect us to run into the sort of philosophers' dilemma mentioned earlier.

It can seem a ridiculous presumption, to be creatively original. Who would have the impudence to invent a new philosophy unless he were right at the top of the university hierarchy? Gentlemen used to do it. Are there still gentlemen about today? To qualify as a gentleman one should have a reasonably enjoyable life. Another division in philosophy, is between that concerned with exploiting the sweetness of life and that concerned with alleviating the bitterness. Aristocratic communists like Anthony Blunt would fall into the first category if they were free sprits, otherwise they are dangerous decadents, infected with moral obsessions. Emotional satisfaction can be derived simply through the advocacy and promotion of an idea. Our idea may be a singularly abstract one with little direct emotional content, yet there is much emotional satisfaction to be got from the mere activity of promoting it.

The ultimate ambition of a philosopher is to be a philosopher king. The masquerade is played, can only be played, within the context of an agreed set of values. To seek success for its own sake is an extremely superficial type of behaviour. Far better is contemplation, but this is likely to be practically ineffective. Worldly success and power tend to come to those who immerse themselves in a world of images. Thus one primary object of the philosopher is to establish a power base for himself. Manage this and he will be stronger than anyone. Entering the world of images he may come to seem a bad or wicked person. Seen two dimensionally his aim is the confutation of others, and he wants to wreck the show.

A certain asceticism belongs to the conditions of a philosopher's (Brahmin's) existence. As much as anyone he wants wealth and women, it is the means of getting them from which he shies away. To other people it is evident that he has shifted his energies away for these objectives. He does not see it like that however and may have what to others seem like unrealistic desires. He does desire the world of success, but on his own terms. His image is that of a power seeker, and he will appear as intolerant. To those who happily play the masquerade he will appear as an offensive fellow. He does not want to play by the rules. He insists on rejecting the value judgements by which everyone has agreed to play and by which they understand their purpose and function. He is a disrupter.

Of the possible reasons for accepting a philosophy, its intrinsic interest cannot be sufficient. Obviously the market mechanism is no guarantee of truth. The majority have conformist impulses that are extremely effective. We may note how rare has been true freedom of thought, how rare and precious for example is a Heraclitus. This is the real reason why classical western science is something so much to admire.

The priest, in our normal understanding, has a repressive function. He is a monopolist, he wants to control the avenues to experience, to dogmatise, to suppress heretical opinion. His alliance with the philosopher may happen when heretical opinions seem to stand in the way of philosophical activity. The philosopher may sometimes support the priest insofar as the latter works to stamp our revolutionary movements. Every politician realises that sometimes repression is expedient even essential, but there is a type of the essential priest who values repression as an end in itself, as an exaltation of his God.

Science itself is not immune from priestly hocus pocus. Physics and mathematics employ concepts which defy the everyday world of commonsense, and make receptive to mysticism. Crowley recommends the fourth dimension speculations which were to inspire Einstein. One modern attempt to relate science to mystical thought is Capra's book *The Tao of Physics*, but if it is illuminating on physics, any student of Crowley will see it is weak on oriental mysticism. There is no study of western philosophers, no mention of Kant. Mysticism has been linked up with science before, and far more effectively, as in the essay recommended by Crowley, Sidney Klein's *Science and the Infinite*.

Looking to sub atomic physics for the ultimate truth of things can be fatal. Everything throws itself back into the same confusion. Our concepts used for handling our everyday experience, time, matter, space etc, contain an intrinsic connected logic/grammar of their own. The pain of philosophical confusion springs from not knowing our way around our own concepts. Scientists apply new and special meanings to our everyday concepts and find mathematical connections between these new forms. Many people are happy to live with paradox, and look for simplistic magical style solutions. Science fiction perpetuates these half understood confusions. Thus the notion will persist of unfathomable mysteries and paradoxes, opaque to all but a few top physicists.

Gilbert Ryle wrote (in *The Revolution in Philosophy*)[42] of how philosophy has become a completely specialised professional discipline restricted to the universities, particularly of course to the old universities. The life of Wittgenstein rather gives the lie to that. It is said that the secret of Wittgenstein's great influence lay in the fact that at Cambridge he had access to so many highly intelligent yet highly naïve and inexperienced young men. Real originality works quite outside the orthodox institutional framework. Wittgenstein himself was influenced by all kinds of freelancers like Kierkegaard and Weininger.

The professionalisation of philosophy can seem in some ways a bad thing. How can intellectual ideas play among society and have effect? The shifting doctrines that dominate society, the constraints on thought and freedom of expression, have little to do with the best thought of the day. But modern thought ought to be able to accomplish something.

The use of reason and right philosophy enables us to enjoy mystical and aesthetic experience without fear and without childlike dependence. God, Lord, Adonai, Yahveh, Heavenly Father, is adored as one mysterious who can do harm as well as good. He is the Mystery who is worshipped. The philosopher, Platonist, Pythagorean, Kabbalist, wishes to penetrate as far as possible into the heart of the Mystery. Knowledge casts out fear, it is said. Where there is faith in God as Father there is a state of childish dependence and enjoyment is limited by a terrible insecurity. Philosophy enables us to overcome the insecurity without in any way diminishing the experience.

There are several parallels between Wittgenstein and Crowley. Both started off with a fortune then disposed of it to die in virtual poverty. Much of Wittgenstein's influence has less to do with the cogency of his argument than the fact that he sets the agenda through the sheer power of his personality. Every philosophy contains fairly obvious flaws and weaknesses, a strength of personality is required to ensure that these are not immediately fatal and that the agenda can be shifted onto the problems now seen as important.

In practice Wittgenstein's followers like Ryle do tend to enshrine conventional beliefs. What are we to think of life after death for example? Ryle's philosophy of mind brings us back to the 'commonsense' view that persons die and are no more when their bodies die. But is this even the most natural view? Surely it is a bit of a wrench to accept that there is no form of survival and the doctrine is itself rooted in certain philosophical assumptions. In protest one may feel tempted to adopt an extreme reactionary position and believe in all the soul forms of the Ancient Egyptians. Philosophy runs itself into paradox. We assume everyone wants to jump the same way. But the person who jumps the other way is not being at all irrational. In a way he is necessary. As for life after death, the most natural is probably the most primitive, first codified by civilised man as the Egyptian theories about Kas, Bas, Khus and the rest.

Reincarnation contradicts the verification principle and the falsification principle of Karl Popper. It may be meaningless as a scientific proposition, but as a religious proposition, by later Wittgenstein if we can find a use for such a belief it may arguably be permissible. Ideas which cannot be proved scientifically may yet be there ready for believing if needed. We do not have to believe them, but we may. But what deformation of the believing faculty is here asked? Belief of the status of certainty is only attainable in moment of beatific vision.

Nor should we rule out the paranormal on principle. If it does work it does on principles which cannot be regularised. Hard headed materialism can never be disproved. Philosophy began with Thales saying all things are full of gods. Some recent developments suggest philosophy moving to a new belief system whereby machines are considered animate.[43]

For the age of Horus we may speak of the wisdom of immaturity. Every point of view is in its own limited way sound. Wisdom does not come with age, it is available to the young. Our culture should permit them to seize it. It is even available to the child.

# Notes

1   Crowley, *Magick in Theory an Practice*, pp. 209 - 214
2   *ibid* p. 151
3   As by Bernard Williams
4   Symons (1907) p. 1
5   "All discussions upon philosophy are necessarily sterile, since truth is beyond language. They are, however, useful if carried far enough — if carried to the point when it become apparent that all arguments are arguments in a circle." *Magick in Theory and Practice*, p. 6
6   "There is no mention of *Liber Legis* in *The Star in the West*. ...Probably Crowley's physical presence and personality, and his unrestrained verses, so overwhelmed the young Captain Fuller that he didn't have to wait for the creed, the manuscript of which was mislaid, and its significance at this time unappreciated even by Crowley himself" (Symonds, *The Great Beast* p. 93)
7   eg. These lines from *Pentecost:-*

"It little matters whether we
With Fichte and the Brahmins preach
That Ego-Atman sole must be:
With Schelling and the Buddha own
Non ego- Skhandas are alone
With Hegel and the Christian? teach…"

8

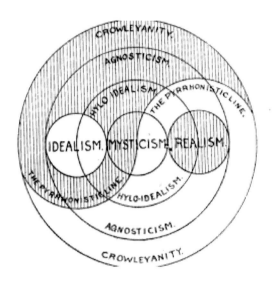

9    Kung Fû Hexagram (Legge's translation) p. 200
10   Scholem (1987) p. 2
11   Scholem (1946) p. 2
12   "From one point of view, magical progress actually consists in deciphering one's own record." *Magick in Theory and Practice* p. 141
13   Crowley, *The Book of Lies* p. 5
14   See E Leach *Frazer and Malinowski, Encounter XXV* 1965
15   *The Bull of Ombos*, p184
16   Pace Regardie who accounts for the changes in the modern world by the discoveries of Marx, Freud and Einstein. (*The Eye in the Triangle* p 499)
17   See eg the Dobu, described in Ruth Benedict's *Patterns*

*of Culture.*

18 "Well said Frazer, the most learned Doctor of the College of the Holy Trinity in the University of Cambridge, that Science was but the Name of any Magick which failed not of its intended Effect." (*Liber Aleph* p. 50)

19 What Spengler called the "Faustian"

20 "Yet, strangely, it was from Cambridge that the three greatest English Egyptologists came, Charles Wycliffe Goodwin, E A Wallis Budge, and Herbert Thompson. Of these the studies of Wallis Budge were the most important for Florence, and for the Golden Dawn for in 1892 Budge had been appointed Acting Keeper of the Egyptian Department of the British Museum, around the corner from the Golden Dawn's London Temple, and had been elevated to Principal Keeper in 1894. It is rumoured that he was not unsympathetic to Order pursuits, and probably aided members in their researches. Florence would have been proud that her book on Egyptian Magic preceded Budge's by two years." *The Books of the Beast* by Timothy D'Arch Smith. –Crucible 1987. p. 102 Chapter on Florence Farr.

21 Speaking of Mirce Eliade (in *The Gutenberg Galaxy* p. 69)

22 Deren (1975) pp. 189-90

23 Gottfried Wagner *He who does not howl with the wolf : the Wagner legacy : an autobiography* English translation by Della Couling. London- Sanctuary 1998. See also Nietzche, *The Case of Wagner*, p. 160

24 Crowley, *Magick without Tears*, p. 85

25 Crowley, *The Confessions*, p. 32

26 Whose founder Adam Weishaupt, together with Christian Rosencreutz, was another of the saints honoured in the Gnostic Mass.

27 Most famous for *The Concept of Mind* written against the 'ghost in the machine'.

28  "Before Hitler was I am".- A C
29  A possibility allowed for in the subtitle to *Liber Aleph, The Book of Wisdom or Folly.*
30  From *Peer Gynt*
31  From LIBER OS ABYSMI, a quite extraordinary 'poem' instructing in using the recommended reading list to bring on the horrors of the Abyss.
32  See Gudmundsen *Wittgenstein and Buddhism*
33  Yates (1964) p. 454
34  Hayter (1971) pp. 117-8
35  I am thinking of T S Eliot
36  "The greatest happiness is to vanquish your enemies, to chase them before you, to rob them of their wealth, to see those dear to them bathed in tears, to clasp to your bosom their wives and daughters."
37  Crowley, *The Confessions* pp. 512-13
38  Crowley, *Liber Aleph* p. 48
39  Crowley, *The Book of Lies* p. 100
40  *Liber Legis II.33*
41  Levy's biography of G E Moore.
42  Ryle (1949) p. 4
43  Dennett (1992)

# 4
# Crowley and Imperialism

Crowley expressed attitudes to non western cultures that are currently out of favour. Edward Said wrote a famous and influential book against 'Orientalism',[1] and Crowley's theosophy presumably would have met with his strong disapproval as a form of cultural imperialism.

If we want to appreciate Crowley we need to divest ourselves of such modern qualms. However it would be misleading to make him into a mere reactionary. The fierceness of *Liber Legis* is incompatible with the attitudes on which it pours scorn, but is too universal to be tied to any particular order of things. A Thelemite does not have to be a Tory, even if Crowley had some leanings that way.

As Dr Johnson said:- *"The prejudice of the Tory is for establishment; the prejudice of the Whig is for innovation."*

Lord Acton put it thus:- *"The Whig seeks that which ought to be other than in that which is. His standing purpose is to effect change, for the past is essentially Tory."*

And Thomas Jefferson told Lafayette:- *"The sickly, weakly, timid man fears the people, and is a Tory by nature. The healthy, strong and bold cherishes them, and is formed a Whig by nature."*

Crowley thought differently:-

> "An intelligent plebs is docile; an educated canaille expects everything to be logical. The shallow sophisms of the socialist were intelligible; they could not be refuted by the profounder and therefore unintelligible propositions of the Tory." *(Thien Tao or the Synagogue of Satan, Sub Figura XL)*[2]

Nevertheless he was with the majority if English writers in coming out robustly on the Republican side during the Spanish Civil War.

Neo-Marxist pundit Martin Jacques writing in *The Guardian* combines an attack on the imperialist mentality with one on the cult of freedom and individualism such as would rule out virtually everything Crowley was and did. Living in the Orient, Jacques gives an expatriate's view on national decline and excoriates the West from a position that suggests Lee Kuan Yew's extolling of 'Asian values'. Against this it may be objected that if personal freedom is a myth, often ill founded, it is nevertheless quite good enough for securing social cohesion. The most obvious point is Jacques' desire to impose his own sentimentalised interpretation. This is so strongly held as to amount to a sort of imperialism in its own right. One imperialism is attacked by another.

It is a natural development for strongly held moral views to turn into cultural imperialism. Many would agree with Mussolini that imperialism is a universal and inescapable human drive:-

> ". . . the tendency towards imperialism is one of the elementary trends of human nature, an expression of the will to power. Nowadays we see the imperialism of the dollar; there is also a religious imperialism and an artistic imperialism as well. In any case, these are tokens of the human vital energy. So long as a man lives, he is an imperialist. When he is dead, for him imperialism is over." (talking to Emil Ludwig)[3]

Crowley lived in the heyday of European imperialism. He declared that he aimed to do for the spiritual what the great explorer Sir Richard Burton had done for the geographical. His ambitions were conceived in an age of empire. In his approach to oriental religions he followed a path pioneered by Mme Blavatsky He understood his own cosmic destiny, persisting through many incarnations, as that of bringing the wisdom of the Orient to the West, as well as restoring paganism. He envisaged a world religion virilised by Thelema, with Buddha, Christ, Shiva and Mohammed, all having their say.

*Liber Legis* is the scripture of a genuine alternative religion. Its position is far more free spirited and worthy of imitation than the supposedly playful postmodernism and deconstruction that has recently invaded the humanities departments of western universities.

In Sutin's biography Crowley is to some degree patronised for a political incorrectness that is dismissed as of his time. We might get the impression that political correctness has become, a new dogma, taking the place of religion, a set of assumptions that are just taken for granted nowadays.[4] That this is not altogether the case may be judged from the current state of so called 'alternative' comedy, where most of the subjects recently tabooed as beyond the pale have returned with a vengeance. If we approve that Crowley worked to shock his own age, we should be willing to let him shock ours. To be fair, Sutin might be thought to be defending Crowley against some more serious criticism. Crowley is these days sometimes denounced for racism and sexism, as if the mere expression of such tabooed sentiments, irrespective of the fact that he elsewhere expresses opposite ones, is something that must always be intolerable.

Not all attacks on orientalism have this offensively moralistic quality. Crowley's approach might suggest that assailed by Jung in the following passage:-

> "I am convinced that the growing impoverishment of symbols has a meaning. It is a development that has an inner consistency. Everything that we have not thought about, and that has therefore been deprived of a meaningful connection with our developing consciousness, has got lost. If we now try to cover our nakedness with the gorgeous trappings of the East, as the theosophists do, we would be playing our own history false. A man does not sink down to beggary only to pose afterwards as an Indian potentate. It seems to me that it would be far better stoutly to avow our spiritual poverty,

our symbollessness, instead of feigning a legacy to which we are not the legitimate heirs at all. We are, surely, the rightful heirs of Christian symbolism, but somehow we have squandered this heritage. We have let the house our fathers built fall into decay, and now we try to break into oriental palaces that our fathers never knew."[5]

Thelemism is an answer to this. In the spirit of Ra Hoor Khuit we could say we gained right of access by forcible entry. Crowley would not accept we are stuck with our own supposed heritage in the way Jung implied. But we should not make too much of Jung's opposition to theosophy. It was not particularly consistent and his own aversion to orientalising was hardly absolute. It has been pointed out that though aspiring to be a respectable member of society he bore a notable affinity to Crowley on a number of points. Jung himself was much occupied with oriental traditions, and had much to say about Mandalas, and subjects like the *Secret of the Golden Flower*. He also recommended polygamy for his male patients. Coming from landlocked Switzerland he might be thought uninterested in world empire. Or perhaps he was just paying the pundit. In his urge to be thought respectable, he apologised for a youthful indiscretion in the form of an early poem in praise of the Gnostic Abraxas, for which he had been criticised by Martin Buber, that firm champion of the orthodox Judaeo-Christian God.

In siding with the Gnostics against orthodox Christians, Crowley, like the younger Jung, was following in a long tradition, including that of the historian Edward Gibbon. Cultural imperialism is also understood as applying to the past and further anti imperialist rhetoric is directed at historians. The attack is launched in the name of scholarly integrity but the effect is to promote orthodoxy. At the end of the nineteenth century Gibbon began to be attacked not for taking sides against Christianity but for taking sides at all, an attack which continues. In his defence we may say that in any historical era there are controversies, sides to be taken, types of person in the ascendant. Thoroughgoing historical relativism effectively amounts to taking the side of the prevailing orthodoxy for any period. Gibbon is himself accused of imposing the standards of his own century upon past times. But such anti-imperialism involves not so much a suspension of judgement as a certain acquiescence in the dominant orders of the past. However well intentioned to begin with, this mentality is anti-protestant, anti-classical, and malign in its implications.

Similarly the leading theosophical principle of the perennial philosophy, the idea that the mystical core of all religion is in some way identical, is under assault from the divisive anti-colonial theory of social construction.

The imperial attitude brings the confidence to borrow, assimilate and transform all the religions of the world, past and present. This standpoint is neither beggarly, nor unwarrantedly presumptuous. With his personal guru Allan Bennet, Crowley made a very serious practical study of Buddhism and Yoga. He also explored all manner of exotic traditions. Some of his practices, which modern prudery condemns are only his efforts to bring various alien traditions to the West. A curious instance is what has been thought one of the more distasteful of the spiritual exercises practised at the Abbey. We read in a book on *Chinese Beliefs*[6] that "*all mediums are in the habit of deliberately inflicting cuts and wounds on themselves while in trance and although these do bleed they quickly heal and the men show no sign of pain.*" Compare Crowley, whose practice of cutting himself in this way might be conventionally regarded as psychopathic. In reality he was exploring different traditions.

The creation of religion is much like the production of art. The artist creates in reaction against the ugly and objectionable. With religion as an extension of art we can see the saint himself as an aesthetic creation. We may compare Crowley's projected image to that of Sufi saints like poet Rumi, or Hussain the martyr. The Master Therion[7] may be seen as a saint of affirmation. In creating his personality as a expressive and meaningful work of art he goes even further and makes himself into a god.

The form of theosophy that flourished in the early Roman Empire traditionally aimed towards the spiritual good in the context of various pseudo cosmologies, imaginary structures of the universe and pedigrees of wisdom. In the imaginative atmosphere of the first, second and third century Roman Empire the Jewish tradition offered all kinds of short cuts. With Iamblichus came oriental theosophical traditions, a lot of which involved cosmologies, descriptions of the universe. Osiris, the dying god and guarantor of immortality, gained a second wind in the form of Jesus Christ. Such was the context in which the ancient world moved to Christianity.

Nietzsche proclaimed 'God is dead' not much more than a century ago. Darwin wrote not long before that. Oriental religions have not been well understood in the West for long. If we need religion there are many reasons for not sticking with Christianity. Some kind of theosophy can surely do very well. It should no doubt be of the most undogmatic kind, but we should recognise that surrounding the central ideas, teachings and scriptures of the major religions, just for a start, there is much worth understanding. Launch yourself into this study, and you will lose the need for dogmatic faith. A walk around the British Museum, that great monument to Empire should be enough to ignite spiritual experiences.

Some seek and discover enlightenment in the Great Pyramid, others see it in Shakespeare. Shakespeare's superiority may seem to rest on his psychological insight, an astonishing capacity to overcome what obscures. Wherever we sense the deepest wisdom, we may yet have strong reservations about certain views. We could not surrender ourselves even to someone like Shakespeare as a complete Master,[8] much as he has to teach us. The same consideration bears on the understanding of other cultures like Buddhism or Judaism. To what extent are we ourselves tabooed or excluded? A measure of adulation is involved in the idea of a genius. One way of thinking of the theosophical is as the fellowship against the stupid and the ugly. Another is that of the transcendence of the barriers between religions. Like the Jew who loves Wagner, one wants to feel a fellowship that transcends the barriers people themselves set up. This may be the whole significance of esotericism. Even if I feel that to my hero I am rubbish who does not deserve to live, the barrier may be overcome. There was an idea of the esoteric that allowed communication between Christian, Muslim, Pagan, and Jew.

Modern theosophy has literary origins. Mme Blavatsky herself began as what we might call a Bulwer-Lytton groupie. The felicitously titled *Isis Unveiled* was full of unacknowledged quotes from *Zanoni* and the *Last Days of Pompeii.*[9] The Theosophist is one who lifts the veils to reveal the *Secret Doctrine* (title of her other great work). Thus it is open to hippies and Theosophists to enjoy churches spiritually to the full as well as aesthetically. For all the priests' insistence on their own truth claims, nothing more is necessary. Theosophy is about delightful things to think, like making your own religion. Belief in God is not an essential requirement. Mme Blavatsky's wild mythology was effectively an extension of art. The Theosophical Society under her successor Annie Besant, with its headquarters in British India, trained up Krishnamurti as a new Christ. That such inventiveness should pass for a valid form of religion, can seem splendidly subversive (though Crowley did not like that one).

The theosophical movement was religious subversion that was both philosophically and theologically interesting. At one time it was like a serious deconstruction, something to be taken just as seriously as socialism, which was and still is. Theosophy has a not insignificant part in intellectual history. A number of theosophically inspired writers have had a significant influence on the spirituality of English speaking countries. One of these was Gurdjieff, a mystic for whom Crowley had a high degree of respect. A writer influenced by Gurdjieff and theosophy was Aldous Huxley, who had a powerful impact on the spiritual upbringing of a generation. Gurdjieff begat Aldous Huxley who begat Timothy Leary,[7] who taught us the religion of LSD.

Timothy Leary's psychedelic manuals have been said to look "*more than a little silly now*". But they did not necessarily seem so at the time, even where they were objectionable to a degree. They were themselves a form of theosophy, variations on spiritual enlightenment. As well as a shaman Leary was a showman, who took advice from Allen Ginsberg on how best to make an impact on America. He has a place in the history of the twentieth century pundit. On one level he promoted a kind of delightful anarchy. This itself is a form of affirmation if we can relate to it.

Our feelings about theosophy, spiritual development, orthodoxy, and the place all such ideas should have in our minds, much depend on our own personal backgrounds. There are very many influences to which a modern individual has been subject. Many of these writers will have had far deeper influence upon his mind than has what remains of conventional Christianity. It is not even that the Church of England has lost all its point. Its very insipidity may be thought its real strength.

Our background assumptions are now more theosophical than Christian but that is not to say they are in a satisfactory state.

Many different answers have been given to the spiritual problems that beset human beings. But simply to point to some mystical authority, Leary style, suggesting the solution lies in faith and obedience is a very crude mode of thinking. For all its promise, hippy oriental mysticism may be seen in Blakean terminology as a new Church of Beulah, effectively a rabble philosophy, something we understand as a form of Christianity. If it is to become Paganism it needs to transmute into a hierarchical one, paying due respect to things beyond immediate comprehension. Leary recognised this, and at one point described himself as merely the continuer of the Magickal current Crowley had initiated. Equally objectionable is the intellectual demand for 'leaps of faith'. This very Christian claim thrives on the idea of the so called bankruptcy of reason. It represents a deep irrationalism which creeps in like a malicious parasite. So how is it to be combated? Of the different modes of access to theosophical wisdom we must determine the one we want. Herein comes Gnosticism with its fundamental repudiation of objectionable authority and the insistence we gain access by intellectual understanding, inspired by an anti-democratic will to power.

For all its vulnerability and the continuing threat from Christian ploys and prejudices, the drug religion, infused as it is with the common Theosophy that pervades normal experience, suggests the shamanism of the people of the steppes. Theirs was not the highest level of civilisation but preserved a tradition of white magic, of affirmative will. This does not mean goody goody magic, in the sense of Christian virtue or benevolence, and has nothing to do with race. They possessed not spiritual riches, but the conquering attitude that is ready and able to seize these for itself, and disdains as unnecessary and abject the humility demanded by those who would have us follow the official paths. Our theosophy has much in common with this original religion of the nomadic, sometimes conquering hordes of the northern grasslands. Genghis Khan, whatever his other shortcomings, was non racist as is often pointed out. This was a late, rather than an early stage in history. Crowley too was non racist in this sense, like capitalism, like Genghis.

Crowley's imperialism was not just cultural or religious. Like Winston Churchill he was attached to the glory and the actuality of Empire. Churchill was one contemporary politician whom he found likeable and sympathetic. In his *Treatise on Astrology*, writing as early as 1918, he described him as "*the one really attractive personality in English politics.*"[11]

He more than once expressed some degree of admiration for the ruthlessness of General Havelock at the time of the Indian Mutiny "*with his bloody sword blowing 14,000 Sepoy prisoners from the muzzles of his guns in a morning*".[12]

In a well-known passage in *The Confessions* he hails Indian civilisation as superior to the British. He writes that:-

"Indian civilisation is far superior to our own and to

enter into open competition is to invoke defeat. We won India by matching our irrational, bigoted, brutal manhood against their etiolated culture."[13]

What exactly did he mean by this superiority? He would not mean what a modern Hindu nationalist means, and it may be hard even for a modern Englishman to make sense of it. Presumably it would be dismissed as orientalism. That would of course be an attempt to push him back into simple values he rejects in complete failure to credit the complexity and subtlety of his thought.

At the height of British imperial power, Crowley wrote that the Englishman was living on the excrement of his forefathers.[8] As he tells us, the public school products who inherited and administered the Empire could never have created it. The British Empire was not built by Kiplingesque virtue, that pleasing romantic fantasy, but by greed and ambition. The slave trade and the drug trade played a prominent part. Much effort, even genius, was inspired by the desire to get extremely rich, at a time when wealth offered more rewards than it does today. Later though the idea of Englishness came to stand boringly for authority and orthodox virtue. Crowley had many complaints about this movement, which has in some respects accelerated since his own time.

Real greatness was achieved by Sir Richard Burton and such people. Burton embodied one Victorian ideal. He was a close friend and drinking companion of one of Crowley's favourite poets, Swinburne, who embodied another. Both were anti-

Christian. As an anthropologist Burton is now completely unfashionable, considered quite beyond the pale. His colourful and often fascinating prejudices are deplored. Crowley of course was no less irresponsible or interesting in the judgements he dispensed. He was not pretending to scientific anthropology. But even Sir James Frazer has recently fallen foul of modern sensitivities.

The England of the 1860s, when Swinburne first published his passionately pagan *Poems and Ballads* was a settlement of sorts. For a while imperialism interrupted this.

It was in the later nineteenth century when Britain suddenly discovered herself in possession of a vast Empire that she decided to conceive herself in the rather thrilling role of a ruling race. Swinburne himself became an enthusiastic imperialist. The imperial mentality had much of a playful character. Its poet, Kipling may well be judged a great writer. Of course the British were not as essentially a ruling race as the Romans. Rulership was merely one thing they took it upon themselves to do. It was not the fulfilment of the one destiny though sometimes sufficiently satisfying a role to make it seem so. The point to make is that in the context of the wider aim, which is almost unavoidable cultural imperialism, political imperialism is merely an incident.

Living when Britain was at the height of its power Crowley took his pleasures accordingly. Reading his life we are conscious of the sheer enjoyment of much of his existence. True he

came from a privileged class for whom the democratic threat
had not yet been realised. Their sense of being one of the
Lords of the Earth is no more. Even where it is still possible
there is no cultural support for it. Thus we participate in a
different culture from that open to Crowley, the age of
democracy, socialism and anonymity.

As a system of government, Empire is an alternative to the
nation state. Thinking of it in its role of conserving minorities,
the British, like the Ottoman Empire comes across as basically
an admirable and tolerant institution. Many minority sects and
cultures scattered throughout the world were thankful for its
protection. National independence may bring the demand for
ruthless homogenisation. Some thought the imperial idea was
a worthy and admirable ideal, and the British Empire was far
from a contemptible institution, though there was a
contradiction with democracy at home.

Santayana wrote of the British Empire:-

> "Never since the heroic days of Greece has the world
> had such a sweet, just, boyish master. It will be a black
> day for the human race when scientific blackguards,
> conspirators, churls, and fanatics manage to supplant
> him."

These sentiments would of course be unacceptible to many,
notable the Irish Republican, with whose anti-British feeling
Crowley would occasionally identify himself. Empire's antithesis
of ethnic self-determination was familiar enough to the

nineteenth century from writers like Herder. It represents a very distinct and in some respects contentious view of the world. If it is imperialism to engage in dialogue with the whole of the human race one must be an imperialist. An empire is an anti-thetical concept to that of a self-contained people. Each has its advantages as well as drawbacks. While the idea of a people can be claustrophobic, that of Empire has a universality to it. Identifying with a people there is always the great taboo, that of treason or betrayal. Advantages are a sense of sympathy with all classes, young, old, rich, poor, and sense that the possibilities within oneself are exemplified in the other members of society. But Crowley did feel himself one of a people and was in some respects a patriotic Englishman.

Ra Hoor Khuit is an unabashed imperialist. In its extreme self-assertion the law of Thelema is an aristocratic doctrine. History shows that aristocracy is in constant ferment. The French Revolution threw Europe into confusion. With it came a flood of egalitarian ideas. High culture had to come to terms with this. Then, towards the end of the nineteenth century came the ideology of imperialism. This did not affect the majority of English people whom Crowley thought of as miserable with some exceptions. Crowley's idea of aristocracy was by no means tied to traditional categories:-

> "Certain classes in England possess manliness and self-respect. As a rule they are connected with sport or agriculture, or are skilled workmen. The essence of aristocracy is to take a pride in being what you are, whatever that may be."[9]

When the imperial venture came to an end what was left? When you give up the pleasure of ruling over other societies you are forced back into your own, and have to try to find fulfilment within the context of your own native culture. To satisfy this too must be able express itself as an overcoming. It cannot be fulfilling to live entirely as is expected of you. For life to be really good one needs to sustain an aristocratic sense of intrinsic superiority. For the exceptional person the democratic and egalitarian ideal is inevitably gloomy and repressive. Thus interestingly there is a shift in the context in which Crowley's ideas are received. You must know what to look for if you want to get what is really worthwhile out of modern society.

Theosophy, we may admit without apology, was a product of imperialism and it was a lot more fun than often admitted. The culture of British Raj was not all as bad as a lot of prejudice paints it. Kipling should not be taken too seriously. Blavatsky with her Mohini and Koot Hoomi, even her dislike of miscegenation, is there to be enjoyed. The comic character of it all was even shared by Indian nationalism, including Gandhi, the seditious fakir.

Following the collapse of Empire the British experienced an enjoyable period of anti-nomianism. As the poet Philip Larkin put it, *"Sexual intercourse began/In 1963"*, which was the year of the Profumo affair. They abandoned the public values of Empire, of moral high mindedness and sexual restraint, and Crowley came into his own for a while, as part of rock culture, honoured by rock stars able to live like Lords of the Earth in a new sense. Ultimately war and revolution meant that a time came when the kissing had to stop, to quote another of Crowley's favourite poets:-

> "As for Venice and her people, merely born to bloom and drop,
> Here on earth they bore their fruitage, mirth and folly were the crop:
> What of soul was left, I wonder, when the kissing had to stop?"[10]

Anti-colonialism, which may initially sound so liberating was put to the service of an all levelling moralism, the seriousness of the postcolonial world, with all the touchiness about national myths. The anti-colonial egalitarian movement swept the globe, spawning the deconstruction which has latterly achieved such a hold in the universities. It is a challenge to reverse it.

Philosophers generally disdain theosophical ideas as unworthy of intellectual consideration. There is no need for such contempt, they have just lacked philosophical attention. There is no real reason why theosophy should be seen as false philosophy. It is not philosophy in itself, but it could be treated, or approached by philosophy. Philosophy may be employed to undermine religion, not only Christian belief, but even the bare receptiveness to mystical and spiritual insights on which people like Huxley drew. However much we appreciate the attack on Christian belief, spiritual consciousness itself, including what Gershom Scholem calls the "*the secularized interpretation of amorphous mystical experiences*" may be called upon to defend itself.

Serious work is called for when we think in terms of the changes we would like our ideas to effect. It is not inconceivable that the new theosophy might one day take over the existing institutions, even the churches. Crowley was happy to consider all possibilities. He even asked Walter Duranty about the prospects for his ideas in Stalin's Russia (the reply was naturally discouraging). Baudelaire said that noble religions have been built upon imposture. We may be reminded of the Rosicrucian manifestos which purveyed a form of Western esotericism such as Jung favoured. According to Crowley, these were documents of the white school of Magick, exceeded in purity only by the *Holy Books of Thelema*. For all his admiration for Indian civilisation, the pessimism of India he deplores in the strongest terms. This is only an apparent paradox. For all the high value he sets upon the wisdom of the Orient, the home of white Magick is Europe.

> "The central idea of the White School is that, admitted that 'everything is sorrow' for the profane, the Initiate has the means of transforming it to 'Everything is joy.'"[11]

# Notes

1   In this book, *Orientalism*, published in 1978, Said denounces the western view of the exotic East, as a place of mystery and weakness, seeing it as rooted in unjustified assumptions of superiority and other discreditable motives like sexual anxieties. Such discourse, he maintains, should be altogether repudiated. The East should not be seen as a separate place from the West. Our postcolonial age should give far more of a voice to the actual 'oriental' rather than to

western representations of him. "My contention is that Orientalism is fundamentally a political doctrine willed over the Orient because the Orient was weaker than the West, which elided the Orient's difference with its weakness. . . . As a cultural apparatus Orientalism is all aggression, activity, judgement, will-to-truth, and knowledge" (Orientalism, p. 204). Accordingly he finds fault with well known literary figures as diverse as Chaucer, Shakespeare, Byron, Dante, Chateaubriand, Flaubert, and T E Lawrence. Said's book is credited with giving birth to the academic discipline of postcolonial studies.

2     Crowley, *Konx om Pax* p. 57

3     Ludwig (1932) p. 61

4     Political correctness is not just opinion, but a form of conventional morality, and Crowley falls foul of it as he fell foul of the conventional morality of his own day. That is not entirely a case of not meeting up to its standards. Crowley's attitude towards current opinions of any form was complex, as I have tried to bring out.

5     Jung, C G, *Archetypes of the Collective Unconscious*, pp. 14-15

6     Bloomfield, H, (1983) p. 87

7     Therion - one of Crowley's titles , Greek for 'Beast'

8     Liljegren, S N, *Bulwer Lytton's Novels & Isis Unveiled* p. 8

9     "Any man of mechanical talents may, from the writings of Paracelsus or Jacob Behmen, produce ten thousand volumes of equal value with Swedenborg's, and from those of Dante or Shakespeare an infinite number". (William Blake)

10    "John Wyclif, who begat Huss, who begat Luther," (John Aylmer)

11    Crowley, *Complete Astrological Writings*, p. 155

12  Crowley, *Vindication of Nietzsche*, p. 3

13  Crowley, *The Confessions*, p. 283

14  Crowley, *The Book of Lies* p. 130

15  *Crowley, The Confessions* p. 118

16  Browning (1855) *A Toccata of Galuppi's*

17  *Scholem* (1969) p. 16

18  Crowley, *Magick without Tears* p. 77

# 5
# Crowley's Sexual Stalinism

There is much in Crowley's biography that offers an instructive lesson in getting the most out of life. This is not altogether true of his message of complete sexual liberation, which is to be taken as the expression of his own sexual taste and desire. The social message can obscure the Thelemic. He propounds a sexual liberationism that can at times seem irrelevant.

When he wrote the New Comment on the *Book of the Law*, Crowley was a few years older than he was when he received the original revelation, and his interests and concerns had shifted somewhat. It is far from clear that the older Crowley was the ideal commentator. In places he falsifies and expurgates fairly obviously.

Crowley's religion was largely sexual, and of considerable subtlety. However, his social doctrine of what appears to be sexual communism seems at first sight to exhibit a crude disregard of the power relationships involved in sexuality. When we remove power from the individual by associating it with some inflexible idea it is the idea that is given the authority. The individual may thus indulge in a certain irresponsibility of action like that allowed the slave with the permission of his master.

*"There shall be no property in human flesh"*[1] is not a saying from the *Book of the Law*, though it was a slogan he proclaimed and is sometimes taken as an essential part of his message.

When Crowley says that not one in ten thousand achieve sexual balance, he implies that all conventional sexual wisdom is wrong, which may be easier than saying what is right. Promiscuous sex can be sex devalued, though it does not have to be. Without wishing to suggest that Crowley had any deficiencies in this respect, in some of his statements about sex he reveals something of the mentality of the despot. Here he is not offering his followers life lived in consciousness of the will to power. Thinking of sex as power is to think of it as a means of ascent to a condition of freedom to use the will to secure immediately satisfying experience.

Sexual satisfaction has many different planes and levels, and each level provokes envy and fear from those below. This is jealousy in all its complex forms and ramifications. It is not clear that Crowley's blanket condemnation of jealousy was the best way of seeing clearly the way towards what he wanted.

## The Abbey

The Abbey in Cefalu embodied an idea of communal living which can be very attractive. From today's perspective the experiment is surely reasonable enough. Thelema was the precursor of the hippie communes of the sixties and seventies. Of course it was much more than that, and survives on the level of myth. Nevertheless it was not a cult in the normal understanding of that term. We are struck by the sheer intensity of the lies and libels directed against him.

> "Three women he keeps there permanently for his orgies. All of them he brought from America two or three years ago. One is a French American governess, one an ex-schoolmistress, and the other a cinema actress from Los Angeles."

> "Whenever he needs women, and cannot get it from fresh victims he sends them on the streets of Palermo or Naples to earn it for him."

> "He served once a prison sentence in America for procuring young girls for a similar purpose." (*Sunday Express* 1922)

James Douglas, editor of the *Sunday Express*, was a sensational muckraking journalist of considerable talent. The other main attack on Crowley's Abbey came from *John Bull* :-

> "In this room are carried on unspeakable orgies, impossible of description. Suffice it to say that they are horrible beyond the misgivings of decent people."

It is interesting to observe the sexually strait-laced react with such fury to the liberated behaviour of others. Crowley was exposed to all the moralistic venom of democracy, 1920s style. Such prejudice affected even educated and supposedly intelligent people, who would often cover their disapproval by denying Crowley any literary ability.[2]

> "Yet to all it shall seem beautiful. Its enemies who say not so, are mere liars."[3]

Crowley's Abbey of Thelema, like Dashwood's Medmenham Brotherhood, is associated in the public mind with the practice of orgies. The orgy is something that presumably responds to a human need. One imagines it could be intensely cathartic. In the years shortly before the aids epidemic in the early 1980s, various forms of orgiasticism were flourishing in western society. There were for example the practices of the Bhagwanites, the 'orange people', followers of Shree Rajneesh. These met with far more tolerance, at least for a while. It is not to be expected they would have received the endorsement of the Thelemite. Nuit is a jealous Goddess:-

> "Also, take your fill and will of love as ye will, when, where and with whom ye will! But always unto me."[4]

Of course Crowley's community was guided by his own genius and the aesthetic and intellectual qualities that lifted it far above the ordinary hippy commune.

Betty May's account in her autobiographical *Tiger Woman* was far from the lurid picture she was later paid to paint. It accords with Crowley's description of the Abbey in *The Confessions* which makes it sound reasonable enough. He does say though:-

> ". . . by sticking to the Law, by training ourselves to treat our sexual life as a strictly personal matter, we abolished jealousy, intrigue and all the other evils usually connected with it. We eliminated quarrels, spitefulness, back-biting and the rest."[5]

Here as so often he is being disingenuous. As Booth points out *"..he must have conveniently forgotten Leah and Ninette's envy of each other in his summation."*[6] However Crowley does make it sound an admirable experiment, as to a degree it probably was.

On the other hand it has been observed that free living communes most frequently do become focussed on sex to the exclusion of other activities. A few years ago Channel 4 showed a TV programme about a commune in Austria, fascinating for what it revealed about human nature. Whatever the founding ideals, the constant availability of sex became the central feature. Sometimes there is a sense of that with Crowley. Here is Betty May's not altogether unreasonable perspective on Thelema from *Tiger Woman*:-

> "The professed aim of the Thelemite creed is to penetrate into the deeper mysteries of creation, and to free the spirit from the trammels of the flesh. As far as I could gather, the method of liberation they adopt is to satiate the senses with the idea of, so to speak, coming out at the other side. It is not difficult to realise that some of the weaker vessels never succeed in emerging, or perhaps do not even wish to do so."[7]

The Abbey inspires gratifying fantasies, as its very name suggests it should. The legend is something different from the reality, whatever it was. Guided by the law of "Do What Thou Wilt", Thelema evokes an antinomian community like Alamut, mountain home of the mediaeval Assassins. It is hard to see how antinomianism could provide the basis for a society. It may work splendidly for a period, provided that there is some underlying authority that can bring it to an end.

Taking the Abbey in the fully ambitious sense as an attempt to realise all the principles of the *Book of the Law*, it must presumably be judged a failure. The important reminder that *"my followers are few and secret..."* is hardly compatible with a new religion based on the *Book of the Law*. According to some later accounts the law of Thelema as practised at the Abbey meant total indulgence, leading ultimately to addiction, tragedy and chaos. It seems the injunction to pursue the will is only workable or meaningful given a clear framework or context. Insofar as Thelema was a complete surrender to the unconscious mind, inevitably this produced an extraordinary crop of conflicting delusions and grandiose imaginings.

One's will is fairly clear when it can be defined by contrast with the moral majority. Thelema is something that others are not. In a climate of antinomianism, however, it becomes the fulfilment of fantasy in a Dionysian orgy of indulgence where there is none of the sustained meaning gained from working in a context. There is none of the power to be got by exploiting the moral values of others.

For the few and secret Thelema may be admirable. The unconscious can lead us up some blind alleys from which we need to be rescued. If I know it is my will to rule, then that is fine, I am the imam, my role is clear. Otherwise my pursuit of enjoyment might lead anywhere.

Invariably the utopian community turns sour, as it did eventually for the Bhagwanites. So too for the Thelemites there was a measure of pain and tragedy.

## For all?

Thelema as the basis for a small community is one thing. Beyond this Crowley attempted to use it to construct a social and political message to rival the dominant creeds of his own era, democracy, communism and fascism. The main message of this teaching was about sex.

Free love is the perennial dream of millenarian fantasy. When oppression is believed to have ceased, that may be a sign that it is actually worse than ever. The desire to realise on Earth a utopian dream has been the cause of the worst manifestations of spiritual repression that have ever been seen. Crowley appears to countenance it in *Liber Aleph*, where he interprets *the only sin is restriction*, in a distinctly repressive way. We see in this limited sphere how a Shelleyan communist ideal can lead ultimately to tyranny.

If the true message to the Thelemite is *thou hast no right but to do thy will*, it can hardly be appropriate to supply the aspirant with some ideal of health to which he is expected to conform. Your perverse, malevolent and anti-social instincts are an important part of your identity, and they demand expression. To deny their significance is to invoke a form of repression on its own account. No 'law' is to be made out of this principle, however.

The doctrine of the *Book of the Law* has a therapeutic quality which does or should provide consolation. Crowley wrote that because of the hermaphroditism in his makeup[8] he could understand women and was able to emerge triumphant and scatheless from the battle of sex. Those not so blessed will look for encouragement and consolation in their personal battles. They find it in the poem itself, but less so in the comment.

Even a Thelemite might easily experience a state of sexual sickness. He may sometimes feel very far from Crowley, impoverished, misogynistic, racist, envious, jealous, unattractive, deprived, and embarrassed. Such feelings may be simply the effect of a frustration which it is possible to remove. Nevertheless for the Thelemic student who feels like this it is intensely discouraging to be told that all he needs to do is to 'get laid', or even worse join a campaign for a future society in which this will be more easily possible. Such advice would only intensify despair. Crowley the man, in all his boastful virility, may appear to set an impossibly high standard.

But Crowley's words are rarely to be taken entirely at face value, and in this case what he does is more instructive than what he preaches. He himself was far from immune to rage and bad feeling. though he often pretended to be. Much of his success came from allowing expression to his perverse, anti-social and malevolent instincts. Having got all that out of the system, love and benevolence came easily. Normal behaviour is for normal people. Crowley was really more like an oriental lord, allowing his violence free rein before presenting as a man of peace. The principle is 'do as I do not as I say'.

Crowley expressed the view that a lot of sex is more or less vital for life affirmation. There are different ways of experiencing sex, however, not all of which are equally empowering or affirmative. There is much Thelemic interest in the life of a seducer like Casanova or Walter, the author of *My Secret Life*. The life of a seducer has an interest that is more than that of appetite satisfied. Much relates to the society as found, the real background against and with which he works. Crowley's own sexual activity took place in the context of what the societies of his own day offered him. Throughout life he used prostitutes, as well as having affairs with native women he came across on his travels.[9] This all contributed to the interest of life. His enviable success with women included the joys of seduction, and also the emotional relationships he formed. He knew not only sex but love. His was an aristocratic path. Sex lives of true aristocrats in all their complexity are not reducible to simple formulae for democratic consumption.

Foucault makes much of Walter, whom he describes in terms of confession, someone who made a discourse out of his sexual activity. One could see Walter as a precursor of Crowley, confronting the great question of affirmation. In the face of religious hostility to the sexual appetites it is hardly enough to be simply for those appetites. One has to reverse the religious valuation and in so doing make another religious valuation.

Some have held that whether a religion is life negative or life positive comes down to its attitude to sex.

That sex is power, is something we can learn even from Foucault, who has had a lot of influence upon social studies in recent years. Foucault style scepticism about much modern science and appreciation of exotic ways of experience have long been commonplaces with Thelemites. But despite the similarities, Foucault shows many differences from Crowley. As a postmodernist he offers a way of being left wing, and making chic a sort of triviality.

There are differences between the sexual hopes of middle age and those of youth. By the time he set up the Abbey, Crowley was middle aged. His 'naive' liberationism we can see as the expression of his own virility, a view of sexuality that is itself celebratory. There may be seeming 'discoveries' made in middle age, apparent 'cures' for all the angst of youth. There may be a reduction in criminal impulses. From the viewpoint of youth age is decline. From the viewpoint of age, youth is formless in its desires. Before one really lived one formed an image of a sexual paradise and promise of erotic satisfaction.

When the young woman is attracted to the young man, it is not necessarily for his individuality. Rather than yield to his power perhaps she wants to exercise her own power to some extent. Fantasy does not necessarily match reality. The reality may not be as good as the promise. It is not the complete affirmation of Rasputin[10] or Crowley. There is enjoyment as sanctioned by society. Unless one can take hold of the fundamental conditions it is not quite the affirmation that might have been envisaged.

The true life ideal as it appears to middle age involves the rebellious arrogance of youth being kept down to some extent. The youth is still much like the child, free from the restraints of experience. The truth comes in a kind of realisation of concreteness as the will meets the resistance of what cannot be changed. The failure of the ideal is good, it is the salvation of the world, the revelation of reality.

There is something very attractive in the libertinism of men like Rasputin and Crowley. A mystic tends to need either to become a complete sexual master like Crowley, Rasputin and Gurdjieff or to embrace celibacy. To become too concerned with making oneself attractive to the opposite sex can entangle in the irrelevant. To become a sexual master he must first become a prodigy of will, project his destiny.

The traditional holy man, including Jesus, if we accept Crowley's ironical insinuations,[11] services a lot of women without forming permanent attachments. Such a life is not 'for all', presented as such it is a harsh and heartless doctrine. However it suited Crowley's peculiar destiny.

On the one hand Crowley's criticisms of the stifling moral prudery of the England of his day are difficult not to endorse, as anyone may discover with a little research into sexual repression between the wars. John Symonds wrote of Crowley as rebelling against a Victorian moral code that no longer existed.[12] That is obviously not true. There was a lot of Christian moralism in the first part of the twentieth century and much cruel sanctimonious hypocrisy. Sexual reform was called for but we should not overestimate the influence of Crowley's own small voice in bringing about the changes that did eventually occur. Changes bring their own evils, however.

Crowley's irony was perhaps only really possible in such a puritanical age as that in which he was writing. He writes of "*a dream of lust caused by the seminal congestions of an unclean life.*"[13] No wonder that this man who could be so outrageously subversive was regarded as such a monster of wickedness. He was not content to attack puritanical morality like Freud, D H Lawrence (in his rather squirm making pietistic way), the educationalist A S Neill, or Bertrand Russell, the men who were ultimately responsible for the permissive age, he ridiculed it in a most subtle but utterly devastating fashion. Therefore he must have appeared as the mocker of morality. We who come later work in a changed climate, wit and satire have modified accordingly.

Today now that some of what he said he wanted is finally coming to pass we can see that a solution has not really been found. This is not to call for a return to any previous order of things. Today's different atmosphere, may be equally oppressive and disturbing in its different way. Sexual freedom has given rise to new and still odious forms of moralism. Strindbergian and Munchian tensions must be widespread, even if the people can adapt themselves to any order.

That Crowley was actually far from naïve is evident from his often expressed views on women, which evoke all the battle of the sexes of a play by Ibsen or Strindberg. He was always conscious of the polarity between man and woman, the battle of wills, the essential conflict which some theories deny.[14] That men and women have conflicting interests, and aspire to different power, presents a challenge. For Crowley it was easy.

> "My will to free mankind is so to speak sodomitic. I want my mistress to be mighty, sure of myself and my ability to master her though she be never so male." [15]

Francis King's book (*The Magical World Of Aleister Crowley*) places much emphasis on the sex magick aspect of Crowley's work. I think that King's interpretation coarsens Crowley. It does not give much impression of his wit or the depth of his culture. Also the Tantric nature of his sex magick binds it up inevitably with the breaking of taboos (something found in Henry Miller)[16] and renders it quite different from mere permissiveness. By contrast Booth's biography of Crowley brings out how his puritanical upbringing gave an especial edge to pleasure.

# Cocaine

Crowley's sense of his own great health, was arguably a result of cocaine use, which can promote a subjective sensation of exceptional, actually abnormal, health and well being. Like Freud, Crowley was much inspired by cocaine and his personality was significantly affected by the effects of the drug. The cocaine personality is typically sex obsessed, but Crowley infuses this with the highest poetry, a lyrical Paganism in which man becomes God. In your intoxication what are you to do with your will, with your thoughts, your exalted imagination? Sex as good a thing to think about as anything else. In such a way sex can become religion. Yet Crowley also claims to be quite unobsessed with sex on the grounds of his sexual health.

One can appreciate Freud in the same kind of way as one appreciates Crowley. In Crowley one notices many of these same features, messianism, numerological preoccupations, sexual obsessions, especially perverse ones. But Crowley is not respectable, nor is he widely upheld as scientific. He is enjoyed for his own sake. One enjoys him as a triumph of will and imagination. Crowley read Freud with interest and couples him with Otto Weininger, the twenty-three year old author of *Sex and Character.*

# Liberation

Many have the same literary interests, many of the same attitudes and feelings as Crowley, yet he was able to achieve far more than most. His sex life was far more varied, he was able to act in an exceptionally satisfying, deviant way. What gave him this strength? Perhaps one thing was his father's religion, another his great wealth at one point, another his friendships with men like Mathers and Bennett. Once he must have been as much a raw youth as anyone else, he was introduced into circles within which he could find outlets for his energies. We all stand on the backs of our forefathers. We may absorb Crowley as part of our heritage as he absorbed Sir Richard Burton and other heroes.

Crowley has many complaints about sexual repression. He expresses the idea that if other people were less sexually repressed one might get more satisfaction. This may seem an oversimplification. That women may not want me is not a function of sexual repression but of their not fancying me. I may be wrong, and it could be that what presents itself to me a repulsion or indifference is sometimes an attraction that is simply repressed. But then suppose everything were to work all right, what then? I would have achieved a new order of power. I would have discovered a way of feeling myself powerful, that's all. All the same evils would still be present, it would just be that I had somehow managed to avoid them.

In any society there are failures and putdowns. Complete sexual liberation is impossible because sex is so intimately and essentially involved with power. Erotic attraction, temptation and release are used to bind to social norms, to coerce and cozen. When sex subverts in an affirmative manner it is because it links to an alternative power source. If one is lucky that is oneself.

What Crowley was proposing was much like the sexual freedom that exists in the present day in Britain and America. It was a prospect that he found exciting from his own vantage point, leaving aside the question of whether that might still leave problems even of sexual repression still unsolved. Coming from a society in which men who wanted variety obtained their sexual experiences from lower class women and prostitutes, the idea of respectable young women becoming sexually free and available was itself an exciting and exotic prospect.

> "A young man is compelled by the monogamic system to develop his character by means of corrupt society vampires or women of the lower classes, and though he may learn a great deal from these sources, it cannot but be unfortunate that he has no opportunity to learn from women of his own birth, breeding, education and rank in society." [17]

Yet as Regardie writes "Many contemporary writers have written meaningfully that the sexual revolution of our time has been almost entirely abortive".[18] He believes that Crowley has the solution. This is no doubt so, if we read esoterically, but the failure that occurred is not obviously something he foresaw.

> "She will take the men she wants as simply as she buys a newspaper; and if she doesn't like the Editorials, or the Comic Supplement, it's only two cents gone, and she can get another." [19]

When Crowley says that not one person in ten thousand achieve sexual balance, this is true as well as false. What it implies is that all conventional sexual wisdom is wrong. That may be easier than saying what is right. He is moving away from "Do What Thou Wilt" to the idea of a standard of health. Given the conflict of wills to which he has introduced us, now he is exercising and proclaiming his own. He is stating the sexual order that he would like to see. Not one in 10,000 achieve sexual balance, he says, but he does, presumably. It is understandable that he should say this in the context of the sanctimonious monogamous prejudice that reacted with venom to his experimentalism.

Crowley needed to find adequate outlets for his own huge ego. In his megalomania he would desire to be God, impressing his narcissism on others. There was a certain androgyny. He loses himself, he does not see himself as others see him, that is as other males see him, as some obstructive opposing will. Crowley's homosexual activity may have related to this urge to bind and dominate.

> "Every Man and every Woman hath Right Indefeasable to give the Body for the Enjoyment of any other. . . this Freedom shall be respected of all, seeing that it is the Right of the Bodily Will."[20]

This is sexual communism. He is turning to politics and a preoccupation with the social message. He is making an intrusive demand for compulsory attitudes of tolerance. How does that square with this?

"It is necessary that we stop, once for all, this ignorant meddling with other people's business."[21]

Contradictions are everywhere. He goes on to say that:-

"murder of a faithless partner is ethically excusable, in a certain sense; for there may be some stars whose Nature is extreme violence."[22]

The very saying that the law is for all is in blatant contradiction with "*my followers are few and secret*". In fairness the former was a title chosen by Regardie when he published the commentaries on the *Book of the Law*.

There is more ambivalence. On the one hand sex is a sacrament, any sexual act, hetero, homo or autosexual is to be infused with a religious meaning. On the other hand sex is to be treated as a mere bodily function, to be supplied in great abundance to avoid getting obsessed with it.

It may easily appear that he is pursuing his own will, that he does not really care for others at all, despite his philanthropic pretensions. As he writes in the prelude to the *Confessions*, a book in which he expresses much Buddha like compassion. "*I don't give a damn for the whole human race*".[23] We might draw a lesson from this, maybe we are even supposed to. Sometimes we should not take him seriously, but pursue our own wills rather than his.

Stalinism is the way of the dictator. The dictator pursues his own course and does not really care for the wills of others. His own individual will assumes enormous prominence, ignoring the individual situations in which his readers might find themselves. Stalin was the Red Tsar, father of his people. The appalling sacrifices he demanded were accepted in the name of patriotism, like the British accepted the sacrifices of war. Political Thelema is a form of sexual Stalinism. The doctrine of complete sexual freedom is in contradiction with "Do What Thou Wilt" in the way we find communism is. It is very like communism in its promise of revolution and happiness that will be brought by an unlimited abundance. That he was not entirely unsympathetic to communism may be seen from his letters to Walter Duranty.[24]

What Crowley implies is that given complete sexual freedom you will be able to find complete fulfilment. That is a crass hypothesis very different from the individuality of "Do What Thou Wilt". From his point of view he is pursuing his own will in upholding it, his own sexual tastes, just as much as when he applied his own will to the seduction of some new flapper. He may be right, but in a sense it is irrelevant if he is.

The interest is no longer in the will of the individual Thelemite, in all the various situations in which it finds itself, but in the often tyrannical will of the Master Therion. His interest is in a social change in which he would take pleasure, and which contrasts sharply with the circumstances of his own immediate present. The immediate satisfaction this brings has a despotic or tyrannical quality.

All the problems of modern sexuality are discounted, in the interests of a state of affairs that accords with the sexual feelings and ambitions of Crowley himself. Some of his own behaviour which was romantic and enviable in his day has been cheapened in these times of mass air travel. Sexual tourism is now commonplace, and is known as nutmegging in South East Asia. Booth writes that Crowley did not care about catching, or spreading venereal disease. This is hard to find acceptable. It suggests Foucault, the first celebrity to die of aids, and the death cult in which he allegedly exulted. That sort of thing is possible, and may even be enjoyable, but it is not widely appealing.

There are many lessons in this. Sex is a microcosm of life, of course, and the lesson extends far beyond the immediate field of sexual behaviour into every other field of life, including that of politics.

# Womanhood

It would be absurd to suggest that he actually was naïve. When he gets away from crude generalisations his perceptions of womanhood at times rise to those of great poets like Catullus, Swinburne and Baudelaire. He showed great depth of understanding in his responses to his own time.

In Baudelaire there is clearly some misogyny. For Baudelaire it is clothing that deinvidualises, that takes away what has to be overcome, woman's own view of herself as she wants to project it. A preference for the naked or the clothed body is a matter of taste. Crowley glorified bodily excrescences, rhapsodising about:-

"blood sweat and cum and the slime from her bumb."

What had to be avoided was the exaltation of woman on her own terms that debilitated the generation before 1914, the excessive chivalry and niceness that formed the background to war. Crowley had no illusions as to the insolence and pretentiousness of the female sex. He was even more aware than most due to his very extensive experience.

## Conclusion

Gilbert Highet[25] described Crowley as a failure in what he saw as his underlying aim of establishing a solar-phallic religion to replace Christianity. Regardie says that the aim is beginning to succeed. The task of replacing Christianity as the myth at the heart of our civilisation is indeed a brave and Herculean one. Yet Crowley's doctrine of sexual ultra permissiveness can seem quite strikingly naïve, with a failure to acknowledge that sex is power. Sometimes the logical end of what may appear to be a completely uninhibited and relaxed approach to sexuality is the sort of homosexual debauchery that prevailed in San Francisco bathhouses circa 1980. Sex can be relatively detached from power, the more detached the more meaningless it becomes.

Complete liberation can be a harsh ideal which takes away individuality and sets up a severe standard disvaluing your own experience. The underlying lesson from all this is how a message of liberation and emancipation can be smothered, how your individual will can be drowned in a promise of happiness that is supposed to fulfil it. This is an object lesson in how Thelema may be misunderstood.

"Sex is the main expression of the Nature of a person; great Natures are sexually strong; and the health of any person will depend upon the freedom of that function."[26]

# Notes

1    Crowley, *Liber Aleph* p. 34

2    "You have read my works?", he said. "I have" I said; "they may be wonderful as magic but I can't believe that anything which is so badly written could be". (Arthur Calder Marshall, *The Magic of my Youth* p. 192)

3    Crowley, *Book of the Law* III : 68

4    Crowley, *Book of the Law*

5    Crowley, *The Confessions* p. 853

6    Booth (2000) p. 397

7    May (1929) p. 148

8    Combined, of course, with masculinity 'above the normal' see Crowley, The *Confessions* p. 45)

9    I would have quoted his Nepali love song on 'kissable Tarshitering', but the sex of this person is not unambiguously established.

10   Crowley was once dubbed 'Le Rasputin Anglais' by a French publication. See Symonds (1951) p. 170

11   See Crowley, *The Gospel according to George Bernard Shaw*:- "We cannot doubt then that the object of all these women was to repair the deficiencies of their husbands; and we cannot doubt that in this case they were disappointed. Jesus of course could hardly have failed to understand their desires; but he knew how to soothe

their feelings without yielding to their wishes, for they never ceased to follow him." See *Crowley on Christ* p. 120

12  Symonds (1989) p. vii

13  Crowley, *Liber Aleph* p. 10

14  In the 1936 "the occupants the other apartments in the building protested vociferously at the stench of Crowley's incense and the noise emanating from his flat, of his arguing with women who screamed and shouted back at him". Booth (2000) p. 460-1

15  Journal entry, 5th July 1920 p. 201

16  Who for this reason did not welcome the hippy movement.

17  Crowley, *The Confessions* p. 111

18  Regardie (1970) p. 448.

19  Crowley, *The Law is For All*, p. 100

20  Crowley, *Liber Aleph* p. 34

21  Crowley, *The Law is For All*, p. 89

22  Ibid p. 99

23  Crowley, *The Confessions*, p. 23

24  He "contacted him about this time [1934] concerning an idea he had come up with of giving the Bolsheviks a 'substitute for the God they have spurned', namely himself, Aleister Crowley". See S J Taylor, *Stalin's Apologist* p. 249)

25  Highet (1957) *p. 156*

26  Crowley, *The Law is for All*, p. 101

# 6

# Aleister Crowley As Guru[1]

Official culture does not take Aleister Crowley at all seriously these days, but the issues he arouses, and the things he writes about, are often very similar to others which are taken very seriously indeed. Take for example the writings of one of the most revered of modern philosophers, Ludwig Wittgenstein. In his book, *Culture and Value*, translated by Peter Winch, Wittgenstein appears as guru, with views and observations on all manner of subjects over and above the strictly philosophical ones which made his reputation. If it is acceptable to study this sort of thing, Aleister Crowley offers comparable intellectual meat to chew on, fascinating, creative and original speculations, normally censored out of the English scholarly tradition. Why pay attention to one set of ideas rather than to another? This is the question of authority. Why Wittgenstein rather than Marx, Freud, Heidegger, or even Crowley?

Crowley shared with Wittgenstein the urge to submerge others in his own will, to overcome their alienness by dominating and influencing them. Both sought and found fanatical followers among brilliant, unstable undergraduates from Oxford and

Cambridge. Through these was hope of influencing the cultural mainstream. However, just as Wittgenstein rejected the idea that his influence should be restricted to academics, so Crowley repudiates any suggestion that he is speaking to some class restricted in scope. As much as to the fortunate members of society he addresses himself to paupers and to prisoners. He is concerned to influence individual minds through unofficial channels, bringing creative thinking to those normally felt to have no right to it.

He did aspire to a popular following, partly for energy, partly as the most obvious possibility of effecting change. He made use of existing occultist movements to refine them and to exercise his will to power. Though 'against the people', the individual who can lead a mass movement acquires freedom of action, and the dominant forces of the day no longer obstruct and oppose him. With the inertia of the mass behind him, he has support for whatever he wants to do. Even a rational ideal could do with a popular base, especially if it is expected to make any serious difference to society.

In 1911 he was advertising his publications *Equinox* and *777*, textbook of the Crowleyan Kabbala, in the *Occult Review*. These were the waters in which he fished, as Lenin and Mao in those of revolutionary tradition, and Wittgenstein among philosophy students. Crowley showed little interest in politics. From his viewpoint political interests may be thought of as a kind of vice, constricting into immediate place and time. By contrast he invites into some very exotic traditions, exploring the wisdom and experience of civilisations very remote from his own. His literary style has an oriental, very knowing, quality. Little is argued, or attempted to be argued. He writes from a position of assumed enlightenment, though he is far from narrow or dogmatic. Also he was a master of image manipulation, a subject of ever increasing importance in the modern world. A large part of his message actually consisted in the creation of his image. For a seeker after power who was also a serious intellectual, the field of people looking for esoteric wisdom had something promising to it. The world of the philosopher and the world of images might seem to be very different, but if the philosopher desires influence he may have to take account of this other world.

Preoccupation with images may suggest corruption of feeling, or at best triviality, like an excessive concern with clothing. The world of images promises the excitement of the superficial, with immediate opportunities for emotional stimulation and satisfaction. This is the world of Hitler as Fuhrer, and that of American advertising and propaganda. The subject includes the emotional power of archetypes and stereotypes, sexual adornment and attraction, kings, queens, gods, goddesses, demons, vampires, maenads, angels, nymphs.

Actors apply their skills to see other people in terms of images; studying image manipulation, they may live out their own lives in such a world. Image contrasts with reality, for example the image of a philosopher versus the reality of a philosopher. Image manipulation appears as a form of play. One takes pleasure in the promotion of a certain image or reputation, and responding to the images projected by others as the truly real as if this is the true game of life, its real meaning. Focussing on the emotional impact of a stereotype, all the charge associated with it, the aspiring magus aims to be more than human in embodying some attractive image.

Certain writers have significantly influenced this intersection between thought and image. In the early years of the century, the influence of Dostoyevsky was strong in Germany, as well as in Russia. Dostoyevsky stimulated a will to believe in the exciting personal relationships, and daemonic influences that he described. This created a demand, which came to be met, ultimately giving rise to such charismatic beings as Rasputin and Hitler. Crowley thrived in a similarly motivated atmosphere among susceptible circles in England and elsewhere.

Where the objective is power and overcoming, it is not enough to be seen as embodying some image or other, as if life were some form of stage play or masquerade. Jacques, in *As You Like It* says that "*All the world's a stage*", but his is the viewpoint of a gloomy misanthrope. Life as masquerade is a limiting perspective. The person who desires power will only value it from the point of view of what he can get out of it. Crowley's first object was to get people to listen to what he had to say. The ideal of the masquerade depends on mutual courtesy and respect, which is to say a general propping up of illusions. A politician or philosopher who wants to exert an original influence will want to spoil other people's games.

According to the rules of ordinary life, success follows according to a given procedure. To raise the question of what rule we ought to follow introduces complication. If you seek to question the rule you will have nearly all those who have prospered by it against you.

John Symonds' book *The Great Beast*, reached a generation of readers in the post 1945 age of mass culture. Its effect was to contribute to a reaction against that culture, but it was also a product of it. Crowley's influence was initially transmitted largely through that book. Reflecting on what he achieved suggests what else might be done. Thinking of modern culture and the normal ways in which it is transmitted, mass media, music industry, universities, art schools, political parties, publishing houses, Aleister Crowley is not supposed to count for very much.

There is seeming justification in the nature of his following. Despite his enormous intellectual power, his initial attraction to any one, does not lie in the answers he gives to intellectual problems. People are attracted to Crowley for reasons other than an appreciation of the sublime poetry of the *Book of the Law*, the intricacies of the Crowleyan Kabbala, or the other profound and fascinating ideas to be found in his writings. Whatever it is that attracts, attracts all kinds of people. This may appear to his intellectual discredit. There is an interesting question in the relation of his guru image to the quality of his message. The same applies to Wittgenstein. The message on all levels springs from a strong, conscious drive for power, and is in no way weakened or invalidated by that.

Crowley's admirers in modern society are from many walks of life, from the insane and the incarcerated, through the respectable working and middle classes, to the aristocracy and the intelligentsia. Among his proclaimed followers are some with disagreeable forms of mental disturbance. Some like to inspire fear, if they can, the sadistic and pathologically aggressive. There are the self-consciously malevolent and the criminals. They usually lack Crowley's sense of humour and his wit. His own hostility was meant as a way to repel fools. People pursue their ways of life usually unaware of the rationale that lies behind them. Hence the value of devils like Crowley to disturb.

His influence stretches among ordinary working people, as he said he wanted in *Magick in Theory and Practice*. His admirers have included hippies, punk rockers, readers of science fiction, football fans. A bookcase full of Crowleyana, is a sight occasionally to be seen in the most unexpected places. He is not without appeal in the suburbs, among middle class women, interested in magic and the occult, people that might normally be thought of as thoroughly bourgeois. Crowley as a hobby for the respectable may sound odd. Isn't he a revolutionary, doesn't he appeal to the discontented? But when we talk about bourgeois values we are talking about something fundamental. What could anyone put in their place? There is a poetry of the suburbs, with its cranks and cults, and housewives. Though one may feel that Thelemism is really revolutionary, one cannot object to its existence on that level. After all, what use do the intellectuals make of it?

Crowley created a persona for himself of omnipotent ego, the actualisation of "Do What Thou Wilt". Living in a way that was outrageous to the people of his day, he crops up as one of the most striking bridges between the old culture and the new, one whose place is not fully recognised in the life of his own generation, yet whose influence is long reaching, out of the heyday of the imperial era into modern mass society, the post imperial pop age. Few bridge that gap; Dali is another who does. Dali & Crowley were two of a kind, monstrous egos, they have been called. Neither will win the complete approbation of the conventional, Crowley in particular because of his comprehensive flouting of moral taboos. There is a great discordance between his portrayal of himself as the wise and virtuous King Lamus, and his real untrustworthiness. This very untrustworthiness is part of his message to the world, and does much to prove his seriousness. To maintain a positive personal image by continuously observing some code, even if only one of honour and decency, is an easy way out for anyone. The path of dishonour is the way to search out the deeper questions of value and the worth of life, it is that of the religious reformer. The Christ chose dishonour, and was prepared to sacrifice millions of people in the name of God, which was his name for his mission. The Crowley's dishonourable acts were not meannesses, they are witnesses to his sense of destiny.

Symonds wrote:-

> "The sphinx with the face of Aleister Crowley propounds this riddle. 'Why did I drive away my friends and followers? Why did I behave so vilely?' Other people have no ego and are just weak, but Crowley made a religion out of his weakness, out of being egoless."[2]

This alleged weakness and 'vile' behaviour, especially if we want to avoid reproaching Crowley for it, poses an interesting problem. To call someone weak rather than bad may normally be thought a charitable view. But in Crowley's case, of possible motives for his actions, even sadism seems a more creditable motive than mere weakness. On an ordinary understanding, weakness would completely undermine his guru image. It must be wrong to see it as weakness pure and simple. We might rather see him as sticking to his guns, to a principle of absolute egoism, on which it would be impossible for him to compromise. From this viewpoint what Symonds would understand as strength is a kind of inhibition. He writes that Crowley lacked integration and was in the grip of unconscious forces. What is integration? Moral unification and control?

His ruthlessness would perhaps be of the same order as Lenin's. Nothing could be allowed to stand in the way of the proclamation of the law of Thelema. Weakness may be included in this. One would like to do good as the expression of strength; however, one has weakness, that is to say a certain quality of self-indulgence, and self-denial is unrealistic. It may be 'normal' to overcome this in un-Thelemic ways. Some people practise self denial by putting moral restraints on themselves, for altruistic motives. Rejecting such solutions, vile behaviour may express integrity without suggesting immediate strength.

Crowley's alleged weakness included difficulty in earning a living. He survived by a series of shifts. Some things that come easily to the normal human, like steady, regular work, are just impossible for such types, putting it one way they are too weak to do it. What are regarded as elementary duties, if they clash with immediate self-interest, will be experienced as impossible. They cannot do anything for the sake of duty, they cannot sacrifice themselves for anything other than perceived self-interest.

Women who claimed to understand him better than he understood himself, occasionally said there was something in him which was fundamentally not likeable. Alostrael asserted that there was weakness in him, something he did not normally want to think about, and that he normally preferred to deny.

He affirmed himself in his weakness. Weakness usually suggests constraint, prison, the opposite of a holiday. Acts of weakness are acts of constraint, and are therefore not admired. What excites admiration is courage, the power to act according to an idea, the saint, the martyr, not self-glorification in one's weakness. "Admire me, follow me, but I cannot protect you. I claim to be a magus, but I do not have everything under control. I am not entirely to be trusted, not because of my perverseness, but because of my weakness (Dalinian softness)." What is normal human strength that is respected? Dependability, loyalty etc.

Crowley is misunderstood if he is seen primarily as the teacher of a new path to liberation, his sexual Yoga and the Abbey as a means of imparting this, with the theory behind it boiled down to the crude schematism of paths to enlightenment. He was part of a greater, far more intelligible tradition. Thelema itself is a rationally intelligible ideal that goes back to Rabelais, via Sir Francis Dashwood. Crowley gave this distinguished western tradition a new degree of development. The doctrine serves the man, not the man the doctrine. Not every practitioner of sex magic is a true disciple of Aleister Crowley.

Crowley resembles a Sufi master in the mystery and ambiguity of his image. In one aspect, his life is a fantasy indulgence. Many of the most explicit doctrines are only to be understood in the light of the conditions to which they are a response. The entire occult tradition is something complex like this. Magick is the satisfaction of desire, that is its whole concern, and desires vary from person to person. A magus combines knowledge with personal development, specific techniques that may be taught have greater or lesser value, take them or leave them, dependent on the individual. A magus will explore and understand different systems of attainment which will be suitable to different people at different times and places. No one of these is to be seen as his central message unless he is a social, religious, or cultural reformer, which he might well be, but we trivialise Crowley if we see him primarily thus.

Social mores change, what remains constant is the will to power. Generally the Thelemite rebels against the prevailing mores. In one age asceticism is appropriate, in another lechery. Crowley's sensual extravagance is admirable from his viewpoint, but to expect it to become socially acceptable is unreasonable. Prejudice against it is not irrational, it springs from honest self-interest. Who can feel pride in himself if an ideal is held up for his admiration which seems to overthrow all the fixed standards by which he finds his feet, an ideal that can easily be copied by people he may not want to admire, violent criminals, effeminate homosexuals and hopeless drug addicts?

Sensual desire can overthrow the judgement. Begin believing that total sensual satisfaction is the ideal and one is as if hooked on a drug, one feels forced to respect and admire those one wants to despise. It is wisdom that is really the ideal, but it is easy to confuse wisdom with its outer husk or shell, the manifestation it takes in some particular era.

The superman in the form of Sanine,[3] or the Master Therion, is someone above all the normal problems of life, powerful, resourceful and superabundantly healthy. Crowley often chose to present himself thus. His life conflicts are described in a context of the noblest idealism. He has no hang-ups, no bitterness, envy or hatred; presumably why Symonds says he was surprisingly un-introspective.[4] His nobility, his supermanhood, is preserved by the externalisation of all his problems. He presents himself as a practical and efficient man of action.

There is a paradox in the superman persona. He is the serpent in lion's clothing. The serpent was the subtlest beast of the field. The lion, as king of beasts, represents conventional moral strength. It does not admit to weakness or resentment as elements in its character. The later Goethe projected a leonine image. However the lion is too stupid to become the superman. The superman has grown outside conventional values, and this is how he has mastered them. He has grown outside them because he has rejected them, and he has done this because he has suffered from them. In the process of overcoming this oppression, he has broken the code most thoroughly and comprehensively. Nothing has stood in his way, neither justice, loyalty, nor common decency. If he now dons the mantle of superior virtue, this is because he is able to rationalise the path he has taken in terms of duty to God, or some other externalisation.

In contrast to Symonds, Susan Roberts' biography of Crowley, *The Magician of the Golden Dawn*, is a presentation of the superman persona. In a way, to take that persona at face value diminishes it, reduces to the leonine, cuts him down to size. But it does give a useful perspective. Dali's egomania took a different form. Roberts' biography paradoxically brings Crowley down to earth, it makes him seem less incommensurable with other people. Much of this apparent superiority is due to this presenting as manifestations of mere Saninian strength what was far more likely to be the manifestation of a violent reaction against weakness. The manifestation, be it strength or weakness, has itself the power and mystery of art. There is no art apart from profound discontent with conventional values. The great artist is not some kind of Olympian superadult, giving people superior toys to play with, from his position of serene mature wisdom and insight. He is one trying hard to enjoy himself. It is not that he has surpassed conventional happiness, not that he is so abundant in it that he creates more of it. His strength is not superhuman. He is driven by his discontent, his dissatisfaction with conventional values, ordinary roads to fulfilment and happiness, to remould them, to remake them so they can serve his purposes properly.

The yellow press was of great help to Crowley in promoting a superman image. The building up of a devil figure can produce an object of admiration and identification for those who despise the values of those who create it. The devil is a hate object compounded of insecurities. Symonds' expressed opposition to Crowley is apparently quite fundamental, it seems to be of someone belonging to an opposite camp, like an ideological enemy. The effect, however, is that Symonds with his moralising is like the straight man of a pair of comedians. Conventional newspaper morality sets off Crowley's eccentricity very well. Crowley makes us laugh, and this can be built on. It is a form of illumination.

The reality of people like Crowley is that they react as they do by sheer reflex action. In the process of reacting they are creative. For those who are on his side, he is a solace and an encouragement, his superhuman legend more than his reality. All his actions take on a special heroic quality, as if they are messages, as if everything he does is part of a deliberately created work of art. Usually they just spring from the necessity of his position. Moves of desperation seem like acts of great evil and perversity.

Hero worship of Crowley involves the constant assumption of his superior wisdom, as if all of his interests had some profounder significance. Always there is his assumption of esoteric, initiated knowledge, guruhood. There is special value in having instruction from a guru. In the study of secret wisdom one needs to be led through the profoundest paradox, keeping trust unswerving. A guru may be living or dead. Crowley of course is dead. Are not the works of the sages, in Chuang Tsu's phrase *"the lees and the scum of bygone men"*? But books these days can preserve more than that. We can even hear his voice, see his portrait.

Rather than that Crowley was dishonest in he way he presented himself, it is more likely that he expected his intelligent readers to be able to read between the lines. The devil image is really far more attractive than the lion. The lion image is less a source of wonder because it is more transparent. As for Crowley's family life, that is hardly so bizarre as it once seemed, as many of us discover from our own experience. Much of his outrageousness is fairly ordinary if we take a broad perspective, and cease to think only of the respectable middle classes.

There are many possible attitudes towards moral rules. Where a moral code provides a standard by which the success or otherwise of a course of action is to be judged, change the standard and you read an entirely different story. The moral code, or the standard, is entirely a question of interpretation, it does not have to be consciously in the minds of any of the actors in the drama. Thus your actions may very easily have more significance than you understand at the time. At the time, for example, you may feel very insecure about your code of values. You may feel shame and guilt, which is dissipated in retrospect, as you understand that you could not have done otherwise than as you did.

The roots of the creative personality lie in the great mass of disorderly material from childhood onwards. His task is the imposition of order upon disorderly material. Much of this is to be found in the writings of Aleister Crowley. His genius lives on, resisting judgement, through the power of will. Judgement (Geburah on the Tree of Life), until you have won its favour, is a kind of death. A claim to greatness is not an appeal to judgement.

In presenting oneself as capable now, one must acknowledge that once one was incapable. That is one's true history, and resulted in a certain amount of abnormality. Only in the light of this admission can the reality become intelligible or admirable. In applying the law of *"Do What Thou Wilt"*, it must be understood what phantoms one fought and is still fighting, in what exactly one's strength should consist. In a general sense, it consists in not submitting to alien judgements and never having done so. Crowley emphasises some of the vices in his own character, to the point where they make us laugh, and seem an expression of freedom.

His alleged crimes and weaknesses include letting Mudd and Leah starve. But I am not my brother's keeper. Why should he have accepted the responsibility of supporting them as if they were his family? They were not his children. He had to consider his own survival first, and that was at times difficult. He is accused of self-indulgence. He was not able to support, materially, all the various weaklings who crossed his path. Did he ever imply, misleadingly, that he could? Unlike Bhagwan, or the Scientologists, his organisation offered no security to its members. Unfortunately, the law of *"Do What Thou Wilt"* did not work well for some people. Too many came to bad ends, seeming damnation. Crowley appeared to be preaching a philosophy of dangerous bohemianism. Why did his personality appear to drive women mad? He never went to prison, though he came close to it once. He has been reproached for his behaviour on the mountain, for an incompletely cut ice step, and for not going out to search for the missing people. Was that funk? He may have been guilty of trying to justify himself after the event, of self-justification in the face of crimes and weakness.

Crowley the Beast made a morality out of immorality. It is shocking that madness and suicide should so follow in his wake. It shows how far he was from being the King Lamus figure he sometimes projected. But this shockingness also seems to express some teaching, perhaps a mystical message worth meditating upon. Crowley lived out his Beast role. As to the Beast, one is not called to an *Imitatio Crowleyi*. Not having that historical role to play, one does not have to be utterly callous and selfish to all one's friends and lovers. One can be inspired by it, without feeling any need to imitate it.

Youthful fascination for Crowley is an essentially statistical phenomenon. A proportion of young people who read *The Great Beast* would feel a close identification with him. Because they feel as they do they also feel a sense of superiority, of being in possession of some superior insight. Not that, at their age, their insight could be any greater than the man chosen by Crowley himself to be his biographer. The Crowley discovered at age 14, can continue to have profound value and significance throughout life. His appeal is far more than something merely adolescent. Crowley was a deliverer from *weltschmerz*, he represented affirmation in a strong form.

According to the central Gnostic myth of Ialdabaoth, which was one component in the Crowleyan synthesis, the forces of unenlightenment are represented by the God of the orthodox, renamed Ialdabaoth. He falsely and ignorantly claims to be the one true God. In reality he is the demiurge who works to keep man away from the light. The difficult task of defeating him thus becomes the highest aim of life. Someone who sees life like this will get pleasure from overcoming the resistance presented by the constant pressure that is upon him to think and feel other than as he wants to think and feel. For him life is a constant struggle against the zeitgeist, a form of war.

In the war against Ialdabaoth, as in all wars, sometimes extreme measures are necessary. Oppression by the zeitgeist continues, whether we feel it as Christianity, Grundyism, capitalism, socialism, materialism, democracy, or whatever. It is all too easy to pick on one of these, identifying most strongly with its enemies, fervently denouncing it as the heart and essence of an evil that really runs much deeper.

## Notes

1    This article was first published in 1994 in *Chaos International* Issue No. 17

2    Crowley, *The Confessions*, p. 20. Introductory remark by John Symonds

3    *Sanine* - eponymous hero of a novel by Arstibashyev, a Russian portrayal of a Nietzschean superman from a largely sexual angle.

4    *Ibid* p. 23

# Bibliography

Some Books by Aleister Crowley

*Magick in Theory and Practice* New York : Dover, 1976.

*The Book of Lies* Ilfracombe: Haydn Press, 1962.

*Liber Aleph, or the Book of Wisdom or Folly* West Point, Cal.: Thelema Publishing Co. 1962.

*The Confessions* London : Routledge and Kegan Paul, 1979.

*The Holy Books of Thelema* New York, 1989.

*Magick without Tears* St. Paul: Llewellyn Publications, 1973.

*The Magical Record of the Beast 666* : the diaries of Aleister Crowley, 1914-1920. edited Symonds and Grant. London : Duckworth, 1972.

*Collected works of Aleister Crowley* Des Plaines : Yogi Publication Society, 1974.

*The Law is for All* : Phoenix: Falcon Press 1985

*A Vindication of Nietzsche* Kokopeli publishing 1996

*Moonchild* : New York Samuel Weiser 1970

*Konx Om Pax*, London, Walter Scott Publishing 1907

*The Compete Astrological Writings*, London: Duckworth 1974

*Songs for Italy* London Neptune Press (no date)

*Crowley on Christ* London: C.W. Daniel 1974

# Some Books about Crowley

Martin Booth *A Magick Life : The Biography of Aleister Crowley* London : Hodder & Stoughton, 2000.

Charles R. Cammell *Aleister Crowley, the Man: the Mage: the Poet:* London: Richards Press 1951.

John F. C. Fuller *The Star in the West, a critical essay upon the works of Aleister Crowley* London & Felling-on-Tyne: Walter Scott Publishing Co, 1907.

Arthur Calder Marshall *The Magic of my Youth:* London: Rupert Hart-Davis 1951.

Francis King *The Magical World Of Aleister Crowley* London: Weidenfeld and Nicolson, 1977.

Israel Regardie *The Eye in the Triangle An interpretation of Aleister Crowley.* St. Paul, Minn.: Llewellyn Publications, 1970.

Susan Roberts *The Magician of the Golden Dawn:* Chicago: Contemporary Books. 1978.

Percy R Stephensen *The Legend of Aleister Crowley.* London: Mandrake Press, 1930.

Gerald Suster *The Legacy of the Beast* London: W H Allen 1988.

Lawrence Sutin *Do what thou wilt : a Life of Aleister Crowley* New York: 2002.

John Symonds *The Great Beast* London: Rider, 1951.

John Symonds *The King of the Shadow Realm;* London : Duckworth, 1989.

## Other material

Lord Acton *Lectures on Modern History* London: Fontana 1960.

Michael Artzibashef *Sanine* London: Martin Secker 1914.

Alfred J Ayer *The Revolution in Philosophy* London: Macmillan 1956

Ruth Benedict *Patterns of Culture* Boston: Houghton Miffin co, 1934.

Frena Bloomfield *The Book of Chinese Beliefs* London: Arrow, 1983.

Henry N. Brailsford *Shelley Godwin and their Circle* Oxford 1913.

Abiezar Coppe, *Fiery Flying Roll* 1649.

John Cowper Powys *Visions and Revisions,* London 1915

Dee, John *A true & faithful relation of what passed for many yeers between Dr. John Dee ... and some spirits ...* With a preface by Meric Casaubon, etc. ). London: Askin Publishers, 1974.

Timothy D'Arch Smith *The Books of the Beast* Wellingborough : Crucible, 1987.

Daniel Dennett:- *Consciousness Explained* London: Allen Lane, 1992.

Maya Deren *The Voodoo Gods* St Albans: Paladin 1975.

Fyodor Dostoyevsky *Diary of a Writer* Haslemere: Lanmead 1984

Michel Foucault *The History of Sexuality* 3 vols London: Penguin 1979-1991

James Frazer *The Golden Bough abridged edition* London: Macmillan and co, 1922.

Chris Gudmundsen *Wittgenstein and Buddhism* London: Macmillan, 1977.

Alethea Hayter *Opium and the Romantic Imagination* London: Faber and Faber 1971.

*I Ching* tr. Legge New York: Dover, 1899.

Carl Jung *The Archetypes of the collective Unconscious* London: Routledge 1991.

Sidney Klein *Science and the Infinite*. London: William Rider & Son 1917.

Emil Ludwig *Talks with Mussolini* by, tr. Eden and Cedar Paul London 1932.

Richard Payne Knight *An Account of the Remains of the Worship of Priapus* London: T Spilsbury, 1786.

Eliphas Levi *The Key of the Mysteries* tr Aleister Crowley London: Rider, 1959.

S B Liljegren *Bulwer Lytton's novels and Isis Unveiled* Lund 1957.

Betty May *Tiger Woman* London: Duckworth, 1929.

Marshall Mcluhan *The Gutenberg Galaxy* London: Routledge and Kegan Paul, 1967.

Mogg Morgan *The Bull of Ombos*, Oxford: Mandrake 2005

Friedrich Nietzsche:-

> *The Portable Nietzsche* New York 1960
>
> *Human All Too Human* trans. Faber and Lehmann University of Nebraska 1984
>
> *The Birth of Tragedy and the Case of Wagner*, trans. Kaufmann, New York 1967
>
> *The Joyful Wisdom* trans. Thomas Common New York 1970

John Cowper Powys *Visions and Revisions* London 1915.

Mario Praz *The Romantic Agony* tr. Davidson, Oxford: OUP, 1930.

Bertrand Russell *History of Western Philosophy* New York: Simon and Schuster, 1945.

Gilbert Ryle *The Concept of Mind* London: Hutchinson 1949.

Edward Said *Orientalism* London: Routledge and Kegan Paul, 1978.

Gershom Scholem:-

> *Major Trends in Jewish Mysticism* New York: 1946.
>
> *On the Kabbalah and its Symbolism* New York 1969

*The Origins of the Kabbalah* Princeton 1987

Miguel de Molinos *Spiritual Guide of Molinos* London: George Cooke, 1815.

Tom Steele *Alfred Orage and the Leeds Arts Club, 1893-1923* Aldershot: Scolar, 1990.

Arthur Symons *Blake* London Constable 1907.

Otto Weininger *Sex and Character* London: Heinemann 1906.

Walter *My Secret Life* Brussels : Brancart, 1888-1892.

Frances Yates *Giordano Bruno and the Hermetic Tradition* London: Routledge and Kegan Paul, 1964.

# Index

P157
P166 Antinomianism